## TIM LUSCOMBE

Tim's first play, *EuroVision* was produced at the Drill Hall, London, before transferring into the West End, where it was produced by Andrew Lloyd Webber. *The One You Love* was first produced at the Royal Court Theatre, London, and subsequently at the Deutsches Theater in Berlin. Other work includes *The Death of Gogol* for the Drill Hall, and a new comedy called *Amateur Rites*.

Tim's stage adaptation of *Northanger Abbey* was performed at the Theatre Royal York, and subsequently published by Nick Hern Books. Recent commissions include new plays for the Drill Hall (*The Loving Thing*) and for the West End producer Kevin Wallace (*Last Night At Club Kali*).

Tim Luscombe has also worked extensively as a director in the West End, on and off Broadway and throughout the UK.

## Other Titles in this Series

Tim Luscombe

# THE SCHUMAN PLAN

**NICK HERN BOOKS**
London
www.nickhernbooks.co.uk

**A Nick Hern Book**

*The Schuman Plan* first published in Great Britain as
a paperback original in 2006 by Nick Hern Books Limited,
14 Larden Road, London W3 7ST

*The Schuman Plan* copyright © 2006 Tim Luscombe
Afterword copyright © 2006 Tim Luscombe

Tim Luscombe has asserted his right to be identified as
the author of this work

Cover design: www.energydesignstudio.com

Typeset by Country Setting, Kingsdown, Kent CT14 8ES
Printed in Great Britain by Cox and Wyman, Reading, Berks

A CIP catalogue record for this book is available from
the British Library

ISBN-13    978 1 85459 919 3
ISBN-10    1 85459 919 4

*The Schuman Plan* was first performed at Hampstead Theatre, London, on 6 February 2006 (previews from 2 February), with the following cast:

| | |
|---|---|
| ALBERT / KEN / CLEMENT ATTLEE / TRYGVE / JAN CIACCO / PRIEST | Sean Baker |
| BILL BRETHERTON | Robert Hands |
| KIT / LIS / PIPPA / SELIMA | Elizabeth Hurran |
| HILARY / MRS L / MARCELLA | Carolyn Pickles |
| TEDDY HEATH / JEAN MONNET / MACLEAN / GAETANO | Simon Robson |

*Director*   Anthony Clark
*Designer*   Liz Cooke
*Lighting Designer*   Bruno Poet
*Sound Designer*   Gregory Clarke
*Assistant Director*   Sarah Tipple
*Costume Supervisor*   Mary Charlton
*Voice and Dialect Coach*   Jeannette Nelson
*Casting Advisor*   Siobhan Bracke
*Company Stage Manager*   Kristi Warwick
*Deputy Stage Manager*   Lucy Harkness
*Assistant Stage Manager*   Ellen Grove

## Scenes

## Design

Fluidity of transformation is vital, as the action should never stop.

## Accents

Aldston is an imagined name for a fishing town in Suffolk. I've had a stab at rendering the Suffolk accent phonetically.

In Act Three, Scene One, the characters Gaetano, Ciccio and Marcella speak in Sicilian dialect for which apparently there is no written standard. So the language is rendered somewhat phonetically in the text.

[The translations for lines in a language other than English are given in square brackets, except when another character translates them immediately after they are spoken.]

## Punctuation

– means that a character is interrupted by another.

. . . at the end of a speech means that a character peters out.

. . . at the start of a speech means that the character who was speaking before carries on speaking.

## Acknowledgements

Teddy's speech about the Proms is adapted from Edward Heath's keynote speech delivered to the Conservative Party Conference in October 1965. It was in Christopher Booker and Richard North's excellent book *The Castle of Lies* that I read the true story of the burning of the fishing boat, the 'Alvic'. For translation work I am indebted to Yolanda Fernandez, Richard Hands, Robert Hands, Evelyn Kelly, Giovanni Marchione, Ellie Marchione, Tim Morgan and Giovanna Vaccaro. I am extremely grateful to James Lloyd, Ted Haslam, Jane How and Richard Durden who let me stay in their houses and write this play. Thanks also to Graham Whybrow, Jack Bradley and Lloyd Trott who looked at early drafts, and whose comments helped me move the play on. I am also in the debt of the many ex-fishermen and others I met in Suffolk who generously gave me their time and shared with me their knowledge and experience. Finally, my thanks go to Anthony Clark and Frances Stirk who dramaturged the play so skilfully at Hampstead Theatre.

This version was commissioned by Hampstead Theatre. Previous drafts were variously commissioned by the National Theatre Studio, and made possible by a grant from the Arts Council of England (London).

*Tim Luscombe*

# THE SCHUMAN PLAN

Tim Luscombe

*To Fi, Biff, Tom and Izzy*

## Characters

*Five actors play the following characters:*

*Actor 1*
BILL

*Actor 2*
HILARY BARRY
MRS L
MARCELLA CATALDO

*Actor 3*
TEDDY
JEAN MONNET
MACLEAN
GAETANO TANTILLO
PRIEST

*Actor 4*
KIT
LIS
PIPPA
SELIMA SAKARIA

*Actor 5*
ALBERT BRETHERTON
KEN BARRY
CLEMENT ATTLEE
TRYGVE BRATTELI
JAN LIJGENS
CICCIO CATALDO

*This text went to press before the end of rehearsals so may differ slightly from the play as performed.*

## Prologue

ACTOR 1. She's awake

ACTOR 2. Suddenly

ACTOR 3. Propelled by a dream

ACTOR 4. She can't recall

ACTOR 5. The more she commands it into conscious thought, the further it retreats.

ACTOR 4. Princess Europa

ACTOR 5. Daughter of the King.

ACTOR 3. Europa

ACTOR 5. Fairest of the fair

ACTOR 2. From the land of Phoenicia

ACTOR 1. On the borderlands of Asia Minor.

ACTOR 3. Baffled.

ACTOR 2. In the cool of an Asian dawn

ACTOR 4. She abandons sleep

ACTOR 2. And, as the morning sun splashes a bright new day on a lambent sky

ACTOR 3. Gathers her friends around her

ACTOR 1. And wanders out into the meadow, close by the sea.

ACTOR 2. Yellow crocus, sky-blue hyacinths

ACTOR 4. The young women gather the spring flowers in their baskets

ACTOR 1. Crimson wild rose, sweet-smelling narcissus

ACTOR 5. Dangerous drowsy-scented white lilac.

ACTOR 1. They joke and laugh under the potent sun

ACTOR 4. Becoming close to delirious, drunk with the heady odours.

ACTOR 5. While, perched high above on Mount Olympus, Zeus

ACTOR 2. God of Gods

ACTOR 3. Idly surveys these dizzy mortals

ACTOR 1. Laughs out loud as, far below

ACTOR 4. The women swoon, blissful with bucolic intoxication.

ACTOR 5. And Zeus falls

ACTOR 3. Captivated by Europa's unimaginable grace and beauty

ACTOR 2. A stranger to restraint

ACTOR 5. Falls utterly in love.

ACTOR 3. He thinks to transform himself

ACTOR 2. A stranger to convention

ACTOR 4. The better to gull the girl

ACTOR 3. And in a flash appears to the startled women

ACTOR 1. On the edge of the meadow

ACTOR 5. As a bull

ACTOR 2. His passion erect, throbbing proud and tumescent, for all the world to see!

ACTOR 4. The women are terrified

ACTOR 2. And yet

ACTOR 3. At the same time

ACTOR 1. Transfixed by his beauty

ACTOR 5. Hypnotised by his confident progress towards them.

ACTOR 1. With a silver circle on his brow and horns like the crescent of a young moon

ACTOR 3. His heavenly stench, more alluring than the meadow itself, draws the women to him.

ACTOR 2. Europa, compelled to approach the animal herself

ACTOR 4. Is amazed by the feckless fervour of her friends

ACTOR 3. Girls normally of great decorum

ACTOR 5. Who gather closer

ACTOR 2. Jostle each other to caress his hide

ACTOR 4. Feel the hot air steaming in passionate bursts from his muzzle.

ACTOR 2. They want to mount him

ACTOR 3. Mount him, all at the same time!

ACTOR 2. Frantic and sharp-elbowed, they thrust each other out the way.

ACTOR 5. But Zeus has singled out Europa

ACTOR 3. And nuzzles close to his prey

ACTOR 1. He meekly kneels at Europa's feet

ACTOR 3. Lows more melodiously than a flute could ever sound

ACTOR 5. Offers Europa the sinuous spoon of his seductive back

ACTOR 3. And she, grateful for an escape route in the middle of this dusty tumult

ACTOR 1. In a trice

ACTOR 4. Is on him!

ACTOR 5. Unthinking, unconscious, unpremeditated!

ACTOR 2. 'There's room for all of us'

ACTOR 4. The women cry

ACTOR 5. But the bull's on his feet

ACTOR 1. Pawing and snorting

ACTOR 5. Stamping towards the water with his fast-sobering prize clamped to his back

ACTOR 3. Surging towards the sea, charging in.

ACTOR 4. Horrified, Europa grips the bull's horns

ACTOR 2. While a stiff breeze catches her purple skirts, lifting them into sails.

ACTOR 1. The white-topped waves present a mountain range to climb ahead

ACTOR 3. And behind, pursuing like a boat's trails fanning out to shore, follow watery Nereids on dolphins, tritons blowing trumpets and, in their wake, Zeus' brother, Poseidon himself.

ACTOR 4. 'Where are we going?'

ACTOR 1. Cries Europa

ACTOR 2. But Zeus merely protests his love.

ACTOR 4. Her face grey with fear and streaked with tears

ACTOR 2. She begs to be released and returned to Asia

ACTOR 1. But his progress is remorseless

ACTOR 3. And rapid. And all she's aware of is the pounding

ACTOR 5. The pounding of his heavy hooves

ACTOR 2. The pounding of the waves

ACTOR 1. The pounding filling her entire body

ACTOR 4. Filling her full.

ACTOR 3. Then the drumbeat of the ocean's unfathomable rhythms lulls her at last into a fitful sleep

ACTOR 4. Where a breathless dream awaits her

ACTOR 3. As disturbing as it's familiar.

ACTOR 4. 'This is what I always dream,' she realises

ACTOR 2. 'That two continents

ACTOR 5. In the shape of two women

ACTOR 4. Are fighting over me.'

ACTOR 3. One woman-continent is Asia

ACTOR 2. The other has no name.

ACTOR 3. 'The girl belongs to me'

ACTOR 1. Claims Asia

ACTOR 3. 'That is where she was born.'

ACTOR 2. 'Where the girl was born'

ACTOR 5. The other continent insists

ACTOR 2. 'Is of no importance. She belongs to me. Zeus will give her to me.'

ACTOR 5. The dream ends

ACTOR 1. And Europa's awake

ACTOR 2. Suddenly

ACTOR 3. Her vision filled with a thousand stars in a black sky

ACTOR 5. And in the centre, the constellation of Taurus

ACTOR 2. For Zeus has ripped off his disguise and

ACTOR 3. Like a fisherman casting his net to the skies

ACTOR 2. Has thrown it heavenwards, where it's formed a new constellation.

ACTOR 5. The bull made of stars in the sky reminds her

ACTOR 4. Reminds her

ACTOR 3. Reminds her.

ACTOR 4. It takes a while to pull it together

ACTOR 1. She must have been travelling an entire day

ACTOR 3. And they have arrived

ACTOR 4. And everything has changed

ACTOR 1. And she's cold

ACTOR 2. On her back, deposited like driftwood, on an unknown beach, in an unnamed land.

ACTOR 3. She looks around and she sees him.

ACTOR 5. Zeus.

ACTOR 2. Zeus as Zeus

ACTOR 1. Standing over her, grim and proud.

ACTOR 5. You will bear me many famous sons

ACTOR 2. He says.

ACTOR 4. And she feels her belly

ACTOR 2. And knows

ACTOR 4. She knows it's true.

ACTOR 5. And this place will be named after you

ACTOR 3. He says.

*Pause.*

ACTOR 1. And it was.

*Pause.*

ACTOR 4. Europe.

## ACT ONE

### Scene One

*The year is projected onto the set. It is 1935.*

*The front room of a fisherman's house in Aldston, Suffolk. There's a fireplace.*

BILL (*nine years old*) *is carefully sorting stamps from a disorganised pile into a stamp album. An atlas lies open nearby, which he looks at occasionally.*

ALBERT (*seventy*), *a weatherworn ex-fisherman, is whittling a small piece of wood with a metal tool. The wood is about the size of two fists. He whittles mostly to give himself something to do and avoid thinking.*

BILL. Polska. Where do that goo?

ALBERT *takes no notice of* BILL.

. . . Grandpa! Polska? Where do it goo?

ALBERT. Eh?

BILL. Polska. I ent got no page fer it.

ALBERT. Polska? That's Poland. Russian Empire.

BILL. Russian Empire. What about Romania then? I ent got noo page fer tha' neither.

ALBERT. Romania? Dunno, Billy. Russian Empire.

BILL. Russian Empire ent got enough pages. Where's this then, Latvija?

ALBERT. Latvija? Never heard on it.

BILL. It's got to be somewhere.

ALBERT. Look in yer atlas.

BILL. I looked. It ent there.

ALBERT. Russian Empire, then.

BILL. This is useless, this. There's no page fer Česko-
slovensko or Jugoslavija –

ALBERT. Them new-fangled places ent proper countries.

BILL. They got stamps, that means they're proper.

ALBERT. They're just bits of Austria, boy.

BILL. Austria's Austria-Hungary an' it don' exist n'more. I got
five pages fer Austro-Hungarian Empire and it don' exist,
and noo pages for Jugoslavija and it do. I need a noo album.
This one ent worth dut.

ALBERT (*smacking the back of* BILL*'s head*). 'Ere, that's my
olden. (*Poking the pile of stamps.*) Where yoo get all them
new uns? Them all new, Bill?

BILL. Me dad got 'em off the Dutchies.

ALBERT. What Dutchies?

BILL. The Dutch fish'men stayed 'ere in the storm.

BILL *hears his mother* (KIT) *approaching from outside. As
soon as* KIT *is heard offstage,* ALBERT *hides the whittling
tool and the piece of wood* (*perhaps in his pocket*). KIT
*enters. She's forty years old, in a state of trance-like limbo,
with no energy. More like a ghost. She wears several layers
of outside clothes and a hat. She looks at* BILL *and*
ALBERT, *is unable to say anything, and then walks further
into the house, towards the kitchen, until* ALBERT *halts
her.*

ALBERT. Well?

KIT (*directing herself to* ALBERT, *away from* BILL). The
'erring fleet from Yarmouth, tha's all.

ALBERT. Good sign.

KIT (*dismissing this*). They was comin' from the south.

KIT *continues her journey offstage, but is stopped by* BILL.

BILL. Mam, I need a new book fer me stamps.

KIT. Not now.

BILL (*passionately*). Godverdoemen. [God damn.]

KIT. What's tha' wha' yoo said?

BILL. Nuthin'.

KIT. Don't gi' me n'sauce.

ALBERT. How long yoo been up there?

KIT. Since dawn.

ALBERT. Yoor a block on ice.

KIT (*not wanting any fuss made, putting all her energy into feeding* BILL). Yoo 'ad an egg?

BILL. I 'ad bread.

KIT (*to* ALBERT). Yoo din't get 'im an egg? 'E needs an egg. (*To* BILL.) What 'bout yer brother?

BILL. Playin' football.

KIT. Without an egg!

BILL. Yeah, barmy in the cowd, ent it.

KIT (*to* ALBERT, *increasingly dementedly about the eggs*). Why couldn't yoo 'ave got 'em an egg? I got in eggs specially. I'll get one on.

*She goes to exit again.*

ALBERT. I warned 'im 'bout workin' on a steel 'ull [hull].

KIT (*exiting*). Don't start w' tha'.

ALBERT. The owd wooden craft right 'emselves in time, but once a steel 'ull's in trouble, it gets in more trouble . . .

BILL (*another attempt to get the subject of the new stamp album addressed*). Mam . . . (*Failing to keep* KIT *in the room, swearing again.*) Blauwe Knop!

ALBERT (*trying to sound calmer than he is, to* BILL). They'll 'ave gone up 'Elgoland [Helgoland], I'll bet. Be back in a day or two, righ' as roses.

ALBERT *gets out the wood again, now* KIT's *gone.*

. . . Them Dutchie fish'men teach yoo them cussin' words an all?

BILL. Yeah, them with the names. Rijk, Ton –

ALBERT. You don't want to be takin' nuthin off them Dutchies. They're a mad lot.

BILL. What, all of 'em?

ALBERT. Stoopid country. I 'ate it [hate it].

BILL. You ent never gone there, Granddad.

ALBERT. Don't cheek me. Don't 'ave to goo there. 'S'all cheese and dykes.

BILL. What yoo mean? Don't make no sense t'ate a country.

ALBERT. Yeah it do, boy. You 'ate Germany.

BILL. No, I don't.

ALBERT. You bloody should 'ate 'em, what they did in the war. Nah, Germans are wicked people, every breathin' one of 'em.

BILL. Wickeder 'an Norfolk men? Me Dad says Norfolk men're evil.

ALBERT. They are.

BILL. Wouldn't know. Never met none.

ALBERT. You don't wanna.

BILL (*returning to the stamps*). Where they goo, these owd places when they're not places n'more? (*Flicking through the atlas.*) Bessarabia, Herzegovina, Karelia . . . Great big area a land dis'ppearing down an 'ole in the ocean? Ruthenia, Samaria . . . Come and goo like tides gooin' in and out. No one notices.

ALBERT. Yoo are the strangest bloomin' nine-year-old I ever did know.

BILL. Great statues a the soldiers and generals 'oo won the wars for 'em. Where d'*they* goo? Don' understan' the point bein' patriotic when they keep changin' 'oo yoo are.

ALBERT. They ent changing 'oo *we* are, boy. We got the sea protect us. Keep our borders safe.

BILL. I'm gooin' a 'ave t'pretend Swaziland's Poland. And Rhodesia can be Jugoslavija. Granddad, d'yoo know anythin' about Hellas? They got righ' borin' stamps.

*There's a knock offstage.* KIT *immediately appears from the kitchen, now with an apron on, alert and frightened.* ALBERT *and* BILL *stop in their tracks.* ALBERT, *not thinking to hide it this time, puts the wood and whittling tool down where he stands.* KIT *nervously and repetitively wipes her hands on a dishcloth. They all look at each other.*

KIT (*to* ALBERT). Yoo get it.

> ALBERT *goes to the door. The wait is agonising for* KIT. ALBERT *returns.*

ALBERT. It's jus' the coal.

> BILL *seizes his opportunity.*

BILL. Mam, I need a new stamp book, Mam.

KIT (*not taking in what* BILL *says*). I'll go up Mearston Road agen.

ALBERT. There ent no point. If there's news, someone'll come.

KIT. I'll goo mad stoppin' 'ere.

> *Turning to go, she sees the whittling tool and the wood.*

. . . What the 'ell's this?

ALBERT (*trying to avoid answering*). It's the shape on a cod.

KIT. Fer wha'?

ALBERT. Put on the prow. The cod'll keep 'em safe.

KIT. Yoor still makin' tha' boot [boat]?

ALBERT. It's when they're young they learn, Kit.

KIT (*her emotions finding expression in tearful rage*). I told yoo, they ent gettin' in no boot. Not while I'm 'ere to stop it.

ALBERT. Just a little skiff. Fer the inshore. Get 'em used t' the water.

KIT. You stoopid, stoopid owd man.

> KIT *snatches up the wood, eluding* ALBERT.

ALBERT. Thousands a years we been fishin' cod from this coostline . . .

KIT *throws the wood in the fire.*

. . . What they gooin' a do if they ent fish'men?

KIT. I don't care. Anything! Thousands a years, aye. Women wearin' out a groove in the floor waitin' for their men who ent comin' back. Yoor dad drowned out there. Owt there on 'is own. Yoor mam traipsin' up the top a Mearston Road everyday searchin' the 'orizon with some vain 'ope. Now I'm dooin' it for yoor son. An' yoor makin' a skiff for my boys? Yoor mad. 'Oo can understan' yoo?

*She exits to kitchen. As soon as she's gone,* ALBERT *rescues the wood from the fire. It's now charred.*

ALBERT. Good thing I ent got no feelin' in me 'ands n'more.

BILL *is reeling from what his mother has said.*

. . . She's a righ' worrier. Don't take n'notice. Likeliest thing is they took some damage and put into 'arbour somewhere up Skaggerak. Or the Bight.

BILL *can't take in what his grandfather is saying. He tries to immerse himself in his stamp album but can't concentrate on that either. He stares at it, immobile, a trembling mass of constrained emotion.*

. . . See, boy, my owd man, God res' 'is soul, 'e taught me. An' someone's gooin' a 'ave t'teach yoo. 'E'd take me out ev'ry day, 'e would, all through the winter even. We 'ad sails me ma used to sew together out on flour sacks! Can yoo credit it? Not when yoo reckon what they got today. Bloody flour sacks a riggin'!

BILL. Me dad's drowned, ent 'e?

ALBERT (*ignoring* BILL's *question*). Now, listen. In them days it were jus' an 'ook an' 'im an' the fish. 'E'd take me owt in 'is smack – open, deckless thing, twenty foot long – an' we'd 'aul up one, two thousand pounds on cod. Yoor gunwales'd be that low, yoo take anythin' over yoor stern, yoo'd sink like lead. Sometimes fog so thick yoo couldn't see the lantern of another boot till it's on top a yer.

BILL. Ent 'e!

ALBERT *decides he can't avoid it any longer.*

ALBERT. A fish'man gives 'is life t'the sea, boy, tha's the truth, whether it kills 'im or not.

*BILL looks away from ALBERT, back to his stamps. Instead of the previous careful selection of one stamp at a time, BILL now roughly picks up a bunch of loose stamps and deposits them onto a page.*

BILL. Tha's Norway.

*BILL angrily turns the page and deposits another bunch of stamps arbitrarily onto it.*

. . . An' tha's Portugal.

ALBERT. Don't be daft. Careful now.

*ALBERT moves to BILL, puts a hand on his shoulder and a hand on the album, trying to restrain BILL and the manic activity.*

*BILL eludes ALBERT, taking the album and atlas with him. Once he's away from ALBERT, BILL opens the album and the atlas and starts flicking through the pages, increasingly out of control.*

BILL. Look. Lithuania – tha's a good place.

*ALBERT regards BILL with sorrow, but doesn't know how to help him. BILL's roll-call of countries becomes increasingly demented.*

. . . (*Turns some pages.*) An' Montenegro is good too. (*Turns some pages.*) This is the best name. Look. Herzegovina. (*Continuing to flick through the pages.*) An' Slovenia an' Moravia, an' Bukovina's good and Galicia's really good. Luxembourg. It's grand, ent it?

*A knock at the door is insistent enough to wrench BILL's attention back to reality.*

KIT *rushes in.*

BILL *and* ALBERT *stare towards the door.*

*The lights fade as they continue to stare.*

**Scene Two**

*1944 is projected onto the set and light comes up on a basement cellar.*

*Wilrijck, The Netherlands. Night.*

*The evidence that the building above the cellar has been heavily shelled is the wood and brick that lies scattered, half-blocking the entrance. Through a hole in the floor above, moonlight dimly illuminates the space. There is dust in the air, a few packing cases chaotically lying about, and, incongruously, an upright piano sitting in one corner.*

*BILL, now eighteen, is in (or, in fact – mid-passion – half out of) the British military uniform of a lieutenant of the Royal Artillery. He clambers down into the cellar, hand in hand with a young Dutch woman, LIS (twenty years old). Between them there's a wild sexual electricity. They both speak each other's languages, more or less falteringly, unconsciously slipping from one to the other.*

LIS. Kom. [Come on.]

BILL (*laughing*). Ik zie geen moer. [I can't see a thing.] (*Banging into something.*) Ow! Blinkin' 'ell.

    BILL *pins* LIS *against the piano.*

    . . . Hier. [Here.]

    LIS *takes* BILL*'s head in her hands, and speaks with earnest force.*

LIS. Zij moeten ze laten hangen. Verstaa je? [They must leave them hanging. You get me?] They *must* leave them there . . .

BILL. I gave orders. Niemand zal ze aanraken. [No one's gonna interfere with them.]

LIS. My brave Englisher soldier.

    *He kisses her.*

    . . . (*Breaking off from the kiss, obviously seriously preoccupied.*) You are *sure*, Bill?

BILL. Sure as roses. Now –

LIS. Ik weet niet hoe je het in het Engels zegt . . . Ik wil dat zij daar blijven hangen tot dat zij verotten! (*Wildly.*) Ze zijn smeerlappen! Smeerlappen, schoften! [I don't know how to say it in English . . . I want them left hanging there till they rot. They're filth. Filth, scum!]

BILL (*kissing her passionately*). Kom maar. Het is hier best. Kom. Hier is het wel goed. [Come on. Here's OK. Come on. Here's good.]

LIS (*laughing, almost hysterically*). Maar het is hier afschuwelijk! [But this place is disgusting!]

BILL. We can doo it in yer mam's front room, als je dat liever hebt. [ . . . if you prefer.]

LIS (*with abandon*). Ach, het kan me niet schelen. Neuk me. [Oh, I don't care. Just fuck me.]

BILL. Or try balancin' on the joanna –

LIS. Hou je mond en neuk me! [Shut up and fuck me!]

*They begin to make love passionately. A light appears in the entrance.* LIS *becomes aware of it first.*

. . . Jezus, als dat mijn moeder is . . . [Christ, if that's my mother . . . ]

BILL *decides to ignore the intruder.*

. . . (*Hissing.*) Hou op! Laat me los! [Stop! Get off!]

BILL *reluctantly desists, and he and* LIS *hide behind the piano.*

TEDDY, *twenty-eight, enters. He's also Royal Artillery; rank of captain. Sleek and apparently unruffled, he carries a candle. He inspects the room, studies the contents and observes the piano. He approaches it, lays the candle on it and opens the lid. He wipes dust off the keys with a clean handkerchief. He runs his hands over the ivory, savouring its coolness.*

*He starts to play, very quietly and very well, the first Prelude from Bach's 'Preludes and Fugues from the Well-Tempered Clavier'.*

*The gentle music lulls the hiding couple into a feeling that they've fooled the intruder. They are so confident that they*

*begin to make love again, their need to be silent adding a*
*delightful focus and intensity to the moment.*

TEDDY. It's hot out there. Sweltering. Moonlight so strong,
you'd think it was day. It's not possible you could miss the
bodies of five young men hanging from telegraph poles . . .

BILL *and* LIS *stop making love, and listen, not sure what's*
*going on.*

BILL (*mouthing to* LIS). What the 'ell . . . ?

TEDDY. Those that aren't too drunk celebrating their
liberation are having a great time gaping at death. Revelling
in their revenge, I imagine.

BILL *reveals himself to* TEDDY, *staring in disbelief.*
TEDDY *continues to play the Bach prelude, apparently*
*ignoring* BILL.

. . . The sweet sour smell alone is gruesome enough to turn
your stomach. The skin on their faces and arms looks like
it's turning purple and an odd shade of green.

LIS *emerges and stands next to* BILL.

. . . (*To* BILL.) I hope I haven't put you off your stroke.

BILL (*still – just – good-humoured*). Yoo bastard!

TEDDY. Please don't let me deter you.

BILL. Tonigh's a bit off-limits, ent it, Teddy?

TEDDY (*becoming steely and purposeful, the better to hide his*
*emotions*). Put your uniform on, Bill.

BILL. Everyone's 'aving a party tonigh'. It's –

TEDDY. And ask that slut to leave, would you?

LIS. You may ask me yourself.

TEDDY. Ah. I'm so sorry, miss. I didn't think –

LIS. You can find another piano in another cellar, perhaps?

TEDDY. I'm afraid, with great respect, I must insist.

LIS *concedes rank.*

LIS (*to* BILL). Laat ze alsjeblief de lijken niet weg nemen!
[Please, don't let them take them down!]

BILL (*quite curtly*). Ik zal je wel later zien. [I'll see you later.]

*As* LIS *goes, she pleads with* BILL.

LIS. Beloof me! Alsjeblief! Je moet het me beloven! [Please promise me! You must promise me!]

*Dissatisfied with* BILL*'s silence,* LIS *leaves dejectedly.*

TEDDY. What's going on?

BILL *blows up his cheeks, uncertain what tone to adopt.*

. . . I don't mean with her, you idiot. I put you in charge of a platoon to take those German soldiers down –

BILL. They killed that girl's father and 'er brother, an' God knows 'ow many others –

TEDDY. Happens in war –

BILL. The people'd surrendered their village. The soldiers shot 'em in cowd blood –

TEDDY. So the villagers ambushed the soldiers and strung 'em up. We have standing orders about that sort of thing. You're familiar? 'Under no circumstances to permit the public display of enemy corpses – '

BILL (*coldly*). I'm familiar, yeah. (*Fiercely.*) Those Nazis was animals.

TEDDY. I see.

BILL. It's righ' they're treated like animals, and the people 'oo live in this place 'ave got t'be allowed t'feel some kinda –

TEDDY. Fine, Bill. (*Starts to leave.*)

BILL. Sure, Ted, yoo can't un-see what we seen here? What these –

TEDDY (*passionately*). Those soldiers you left hanging in the street, do you think they wanted to be here any more than you do? They were forced into fighting just like you were. And in Wehrmacht uniforms because that's the way the cards fell. Did you actually look at them? They're boys; they're your age.

BILL. They shot 'er eight-year-old brother dead! Let 'em 'ang!

TEDDY (*angry*). Of course! All of eighteen years old yourself, you'd know best. It's not enough those soldiers were killed. There should be more humiliation! And where does it end, Bill? What do you think? The same as before? We humiliate every single German one more time?

BILL. A course not, but –

TEDDY. Stop playing Bach and Beethoven, perhaps? Demand a few more crushing reparations so that some new Hitler claws his way out of the rubble?

BILL, *ashamed, stays silent.*

. . . Not to mention that I could have you court-martialled for disobeying orders.

BILL (*a playful rebuttal*). Fuck off, Teddy.

TEDDY *attempts a different tack.*

TEDDY. Before this war, when I was in Germany, I stayed in a grand house in Hanover that would have been just like this one. Doesn't exist any more. The entire city's flattened. There were four teenage boys in that family. I used to play duets with the oldest. One of those boys you left hanging up there reminded me . . . (*Unable to finish the thought.*) You and I were agreed. We've got to see beyond what's happened in this village.

BILL *still doesn't respond.*

. . . Europe has destroyed itself.

BILL. Again.

TEDDY. Not just the buildings and the people. The ideas that could unite a civilised Europe have been wiped out. However we do it, whatever role we take, our job's got to be to reunite it, Bill. But in such a way that this can never be repeated. Reconciliation. Reconstruction.

BILL. A completely new form a government!

TEDDY. So you read the Arthur Salter I lent you!

BILL. A course! I'm jus' as much a European as yoo are!

TEDDY. You can speak the languages and fuck the women alright. It's not quite the same thing!

BILL. Oh come on! I ent noticed many other COs steppin' forward to debate Spinelli and Arthur Salter with yoo! Wha' do yoo think those berks would think if yoo asked 'em their opinion of a 'supranational government'? They'd prob'ly jus' think yoo were a homosexual.

TEDDY. It's infuriating the way you slip back into the mentality of a Suffolk fisherman. You're bright. You can speak languages men in your platoon haven't even heard of. You've got to hack away at those roots, my friend. My father was a carpenter. Grew up in Broadstairs for goodness sake. But I'm damned if I'm going to let that hold me back.

BILL. Learn t'talk posh yoo mean!

TEDDY. Not just that, but it would certainly be an excellent start! No, the civil servant had it right! Arthur Salter! He understood.

BILL. Yeah! Tha's wha' I'm gooin' a be once this is over. A civil servant!

TEDDY. A government beyond the control of nation states and politicians. Beyond even electorates. That's Salter's breakthrough.

BILL. In a way, *Hitler* had the same idea too, din't 'e? Got it upside down though. Tryin' t'make Europe, German. What Salter's sayin' is we wanna make Germany, European –

TEDDY. That's it –

BILL. An' create a union of equal states.

TEDDY. Absolutely! So presumably you can now make a distinction between Germans and Nazis.

BILL. A course!

TEDDY. And the men outside . . .

BILL (*realising he must take action*). Yeah, I get it.

LIS *enters.* TEDDY *watches* BILL *carefully to see what* BILL *will do.*

BILL *is undecided, torn. He makes no move to go.*

TEDDY *sits at the piano. He begins to play the slow movement from Schubert's Piano Sonata No.21 in B flat major, sporadically.*

TEDDY. These people here are comparatively well off: at least they've got some cows and a few fields. In the cities they eat books, make soup from tree bark, or starve.

TEDDY *looks at* BILL.

BILL (*to* LIS, *apologetically*). Het spijt me heel erg, Lis, maar ik moet de lijken naar beneden haalen. [Excuse me, Lis. I have to take the corpses down.] (*Exits hurriedly.*)

LIS, *angrily, follows* BILL'*s exit with her eyes.*

TEDDY (*to* LIS). He didn't have a choice.

LIS *stares at* TEDDY, *raging and impotent, and hopelessly sad. She exits.*

TEDDY *continues to play the Schubert sonata, alone in the dusty cellar, the music creating for him the memory of a lost past . . . as the lights fade.*

## Scene Three

*A pebble beach in Aldston on the Suffolk coast.*

*It's a calm but cold winter's day, about noon.*

*The sound of the sea (out-front) can be heard.*

*A wood-hulled fishing boat is beached on the shingle, prow end pointing towards the audience. If we were able to see the entire boat we would see a forty-foot, two-man fishing craft, with a stern rigged for bottom dragging. The visible prow is at least six feet tall. Currently there is a ladder leaning up against it, via which the deck can be reached.*

*The name of the boat, 'The Mearston', is visible on the prow.*

*Around the boat, the beach is littered with debris: a black plastic dustbin, bits of styrofoam fish boxes, rope, empty plastic fuel tins, buoys, floats, beer cans, food wrappers, etc.*

*Additionally, near the boat there is a little pile of old-looking electronic equipment, wires sticking out at all angles, together with a few personal items; mugs, toiletries, jackets, boots, a sleeping bag, a transistor radio and a framed photo.*

*A projection tells us it's 1992.*

*The transistor is tinnily playing pop music.*

*KEN, forties, appears on the deck of the boat, holding a navigation device, which he has just ripped out of the pilothouse. He clambers down the ladder with it. One of his hands is bandaged.*

RADIO. That's 'The End of the Road' by Boyz II Men. And now, on BBC Radio Suffolk, the Shipping Forecast issued by the Met Office, on behalf of the Maritime and Coastguard Agency, at 1105 on Tuesday 06 January 1992. There are warnings of gales in Viking South Utshire Forties Fisher Trafalgar –

*KEN, who's added the navigation equipment to the pile, has started to go back up the ladder. He swiftly reverses his direction, shins down the ladder and turns the radio off.*

*He takes cigarettes and a lighter from his pocket and lights a cigarette with difficulty. Even on a calm day there's a wind on the beach.*

*He catches sight of something out-front (i.e. out at sea) that grabs his attention.*

KEN (*horrified*). Yoor kiddin' me.

*He crouches down on the pebbles to smoke his cigarette and stare, absorbed, at what he's spotted.*

. . . (*Mumbling to himself.*) Yoo 'ave *got* t'be kiddin' me. They're 'aving a flamin' laugh. (*Blowing out smoke, wearily.*) Wha's the point?

*HILARY, KEN's wife, arrives. She's wrapped up well in old clothes.*

HILARY (*with forced cheerfulness*). Yoo talkin' t'me?

KEN (*quietly, but not caring much if she hears*). Why would I wanna do tha'?

HILARY *heard.*

HILARY. Wha'? Yoo talkin' to yoorself these days. Gooin' mad, are yoo?

KEN. Yeah, gal, I'm gooin' mad, yeah.

*HILARY's adrenalin is up. She has to keep a lid on it, as she intends to be calming and sympathetic. HILARY has lost touch with how to reach KEN, and is daunted by his mood.*

HILARY (*suspiciously*). Wha' you dooin' down 'ere?

*She gets no response. She sees the pile of things that KEN has taken out of the boat.*

. . . Wha's all this then?

*KEN doesn't answer. HILARY picks up some electronic equipment.*

. . . They want the boot [boat] complete. Yoo ent meant t'take nuthin' owt. Regoolation says.

KEN (*scornfully*). Regoolation!

HILARY. I ent defendin' it, but yoo ent allowed to sell stuff on.

KEN. It's just a few bits.

HILARY. I don't want them findin' no reason for not givin' us the money, boy.

KEN. Wha'? Yoo think they're gooin' a get up there an' inspect it?

HILARY. They might do. Yoo know wha' they're like.

KEN. MAFF men never been in a boot. They wouldn't know what they was lookin' for. Anyroad, this stuff's just scrap mostly.

*HILARY picks up the framed photo from the pile and inspects it.*

HILARY. This ent scrap.

*KEN doesn't want to engage with her about it.*

. . . Where was we there? Didn't know you 'ad this in the boot. My God, were that when we went up Sherrin'am? Bloody 'ell, yoo got all yoor hair! Phworr, lovely!

KEN. Keep it if yoo want.

HILARY. Wha' was you gooin' a do with it? (*Joking.*) Chuck it?

KEN *doesn't answer.*

. . . Yoo weren't, Ken!

KEN *looks at the photo, over* HILARY*'s shoulder.*

KEN. Long time ago, eh?

HILARY *puts the photo down.*

*Having finished his cigarette,* KEN *goes to climb the ladder again.* HILARY *sees what* KEN *had seen out-front.*

. . . Dutch.

HILARY. How yoo know? Could be Danish, or Spanish.

KEN. What yoo after 'ere, any'ow?

HILARY. Been talkin' t'MAFF.

KEN. Yoor always talkin' t'MAFF.

HILARY. No, they phoned us. Young gal.

KEN. Wha' they want?

HILARY. You ent gooin' a like it.

KEN. Don't tell me then.

KEN, *now on deck, disappears from view.*

HILARY. They want t'move it forward to t'morra.

KEN *immediately reappears.*

KEN (*appalled*). T'morra? T'morra? No. Ent no way.

HILARY. Come on, boy. Makes no odds, t'morra or Friday.

KEN. Three days is a difference.

HILARY. I don't know what yoo think can 'appen 'tween now an' then. Yoov done the 'ard part, yoov made the decision –

KEN (*climbing down the ladder*). No way. Tell 'em no.

HILARY. Let's just get the thing decommissioned now –

KEN (*snorting derisively*). Decommissioned! Destroyed, yoo mean.

HILARY. The sooner we get the money an' pay off the fine, the sooner we'll be straight and we can start again.

KEN. *I'll* tell 'em, then.

HILARY. Listen t'me. This 'as been draggin' on too long. Ent no good fer yoo nor me. Let's bring it to an end an' move on.

KEN. They said Friday. It's gooin' a be Friday. (*Starts to leave.*)

HILARY. I said OK to 'er, Ken.

KEN (*stopped in his tracks*). Yoo wha'? Yoo din't ask me first?

HILARY. They weren't phonin' to *ask* us.

KEN. Why?

HILARY. She said it's impossible for them now to get anyone up to Aldston, Friday.

KEN. Not my problem.

HILARY. Don't s'pose they're tryin' t'muck us abowt intentional.

KEN. Course they are, they've been muckin' us abowt fer years. Tha's why we're in this mess in the first place.

*He kicks some fishing boxes in anger.*

HILARY. T'be honest it's better fer me. If I ent 'ere Friday I can make the meetin' down Low'stof [Lowestoft] with Clayton.

KEN. Oh, I get it! Tha's what this is all abowt.

HILARY. Course it ent. It's just the way it's fallen owt.

KEN. Reckon yoo phoned *them*.

HILARY. Course I bloody din't. But it's 'andy [handy] now I can do both.

KEN. Do both? This ent gooin' a be no social occasion.

HILARY. Ent you pleased fer me? Fine'ly got 'im t'meet us.

KEN. I don't give a stuff about that twot.

HILARY. 'E's given us fifteen minutes to sell 'im the campaign. 'E's a Junior Minister now. If we can get the information to 'im –

KEN. Yoor not listenin' a me.

HILARY (*a bright idea*). Listen, this way I could even get some photos. Show Clayton what MAFF's doing t'these parts.

KEN. Yoo tryin' t'turn this into a circus?

*He moves away from her, toys with his cigarettes.*

HILARY. Yoor mam's tiptoeing round the 'ouse, don't dare to be in the same room as yoo. An' for Jase's sake an' all. Let's just get it done.

KEN. Jase? 'E don't understan' this.

HILARY. He's twelve. Course 'e do. Wouldn't go t'school t'day. Cryin' like a little kid, 'e was.

KEN. Wha' did yoo say to 'im?

HILARY. Why don't *you* talk to him? *Talk* to him, Ken.

KEN. Ent nothin' t'say.

*HILARY looks at KEN with amazement. He is equally baffled by her position. They shift away from each other.*

HILARY. Well, talk t'*me*.

*KEN moves towards the boat and leans on it.*

KEN (*with difficulty*). No . . . (*A fresh attempt.*) It's . . .

*KEN is perhaps about to open up. A mobile phone rings. HILARY feels about in her pockets. She withdraws an early-90s-style handset.*

HILARY (*into phone*). Yeah? Alrigh'. Bit busy now.

*HILARY glances at KEN, who dejectedly lights another cigarette. HILARY becomes absorbed with her phone call.*

. . . Wha'? No, if yoo can . . . Yeah, that sounds great. We'll use that. No, I can make it on Friday now for the meeting with Clayton, definitely.

*KEN picks up the photo.*

. . . And I got Townsend at the 'erald [Herald] to agree t'cover the decommissioning of the boot. Yeah, thanks. 'E's gooin' a bring a camera an' all.

*Looking at the photo,* KEN *is moved to tearful sadness, but hides his feelings from* HILARY, *who anyway is still absorbed by her phone call.*

. . . So, at the Clayton meeting, if we include George Henson's tachograph-in-the-van situation an' Audrey Benn's livestock, an' we've got the 'ealth and safety thing with Staples Senior 'ome, that prop'ly covers all the bases, don't it?

KEN *discards the photo to one side and starts packing the rest of the things into a cardboard box.*

. . . They're gooin' a have t'listen to us! Ent gooin' a write us off n'more! Yeah! Listen, I gotta goo. Talk t'yoo later.

HILARY *hangs up.*

KEN. I ent letting 'er go when there's one of them ships owt there, gal. It ent 'appenin'.

HILARY. There's always gooin' a be one a them ships owt there. Forget 'bowt them. It'll drive yoo mad.

KEN. And there ent gooin' a be no newspapers 'ere, I tell yoo tha', so yoo can call off Townsend an' the flamin' Ipswich 'erald righ' now.

HILARY. They're gooin' a destroy yer boot, boy. We ent able t'pay the fine. We couldn't pay it if yoo fished till –

KEN. They ent 'aving 'er t'morra. (*Indicating the ship out-front.*) Not while that flamin' ship –

HILARY. It'll 'ave moved on by t'morra.

KEN. Righ'! To spew owt 'undreds a tons a cod in Rotterdam or wherever, while my boot is destroyed 'cause she caught 300lbs over 'er quota. Yoo think I'll go mad? Too late t'worry 'bowt tha'. And just so yoo know, watchin' my wife poncing 'bowt in Low'stof an' London with Ministers an' Councillors an' God knows 'oo, while my life is 'acked to pieces on this beach, ent makin' me no saner.

KEN*'s finished boxing his things up and marches off, leaving the photo behind.*

HILARY *notices the discarded photo.*

*Light shift.*

## Scene Four

*An office in 10 Downing Street.*

*A splendid portrait of King George VI hangs prominently.*

*1950 is projected onto the set.*

*MRS L, a matter-of-fact middle-aged secretary, and BILL (now twenty-four) occupy stations in a large and luxurious office.*

*There is an empty desk next to BILL's.*

*In the intervening six years, BILL has taken TEDDY's advice and learned to 'talk posh'.*

MRS L. How long's she going to be in there? *He'll* be here in a moment.

BILL. She'll make it.

MRS L. In fact he's overdue. What allows Pippa to think she can swan around like this?

BILL (*casting his eye over the unoccupied desk next to his, and the papers spread over it*). She's coordinating Korea, isn't she?

MRS L. Don't you start sorting it out. If she thinks she's ever going to make it beyond junior officer –

BILL. Now, Mrs L, you know you love her really –

MRS L. If he arrives and it's . . . Leave it, Bill!

BILL (*sorting out PIPPA's desk*). I've got to do something.

MRS L. You've got enough work of your own, haven't you?

BILL. Masses. They're discussing the Schuman Plan this morning. I've had notes from almost every embassy in town to correlate. It's incredibly exciting. I hope I get to meet the man himself.

MRS L. Who? Schuman?

BILL. No. Monnet! Jean Monnet! He needed a famous name to launch the plan, and he got the French Foreign Secretary, Robert Schuman. That's why it's called the Schuman Plan.

But Monnet's the man who wrote it. I heard him speak
about it at the Federal Union. He's a true visionary, Mrs L.

MRS L. One of those crank federalists, are you?

BILL (*proudly*). Very much so. See, Schuman's – well,
Monnet's plan is an idea of pure genius. Takes all the theory
from the last half-century – Salter, Spinelli – and sets it in
motion with a concrete –

MRS L (*dismissively*). Mark my words, industry'll never wear
it, Bill. It won't want to get involved with Europe. Britain's
streets ahead of France or Germany. That's the way
industry'll see it.

BILL. But what do you think of the idea yourself, Mrs L?

MRS L. I don't suppose what *I* think is of any importance.
You're new, Bill, so you won't mind me reminding you.
You're a junior clerical officer. You're not paid to have an
opinion. Look at the time. If that young woman's not –

PIPPA *enters. She's a very attractive, intelligent young
woman with a bad hangover.*

BILL *unconsciously smoothes his hair down.*

MRS L. At last!

BILL. Better?

MRS L. No one would guess by your behaviour that you're on
your final warning. Get that desk in order. The PM'll be
down in a second.

PIPPA (*sits at her desk*). Christmas.

MRS L. Quick!

BILL. Here, let me help.

PIPPA. You're a poppet.

BILL *beams with satisfaction.*

MRS L. You're a fool.

BILL (*sorting PIPPA's folders efficiently*). That's the up-to-
date file, as of midnight last night. These are the telegrams
that have arrived since then. Pippa! What are you going to
say when he asks for an overview?

PIPPA. Bill, I can't see straight. I have no overview.

BILL. The Korean Ambassador says he can't come till after lunch. (*Holding a telegram.*) Look.

PIPPA. Oh.

BILL. Something's up.

PIPPA. What's up, Bill? Quickly tell me what to say.

BILL. He's probably waiting to talk to Washington.

PIPPA. Clever!

MRS L. Disgraceful.

BILL. She needs to know!

MRS L. Don't cheek me!

BILL. Sorry.

PIPPA. Bill, don't be craven. Stand up for yourself for once!

BILL. Yes, yes, I will.

PIPPA (*to* MRS L). It's not often I –

MRS L. You treat this place like you own –

PIPPA. I may have had a few too many drinks last night –

BILL. In Switzerland?

PIPPA. Where?

BILL. Switzerland.

PIPPA. What are you talking about?

BILL. On Friday you said you were going with your father to Switzerland.

PIPPA. Did I?

BILL. Yes, that's why you couldn't meet me.

PIPPA (*blithely*). Oh. No. Helmut was in town.

BILL (*disgruntled*). Oh. Right.

*The phone on* MRS L*'s desk rings.*

MRS L. This'll be him. (*Into phone.*) Right. (*Hangs up.*) Mr Attlee's on his way.

*The three of them gather folders and stand in front of their desks.*

*Now the conversation becomes hushed and urgent, as they wait for the entrance of the PM.*

PIPPA (*to* BILL). How do I look?

BILL (*trying not to sound too smitten*). Lovely.

*PIPPA senses the feeling underneath BILL's response. She smiles. BILL is embarrassed.*

MRS L (*under her breath*). God help us.

*They now wait, BILL awkward, in tense silence for the arrival of the PM.*

*After a moment, MRS L breaks it.*

. . . The arrogance of it I can't get my head around. As if any ordinary person wouldn't kill to have your job.

PIPPA (*turning her back on* MRS L). Talk to me, Bill.

BILL. Erm, alright. Jean Monnet's here for a meeting with the PM. Jean Monnet. Here, in Number 10!

PIPPA. Not about politics. What did you do at the weekend?

BILL. I spent Saturday back home in Aldston with my brother Tom.

PIPPA. Oh, how dull.

MRS L (*keeping her eye on the door*). Shhh.

PIPPA. Why don't you stay in town and meet girls?

BILL (*swallowing his impulsive reaction and ploughing on*). And on Sunday, my old chum Teddy invited us to Broadstairs for lunch. Took us to Bexley and showed us where he meets his constituents. It's incredibly exciting –

MRS L (*about the* PM). Quiet. I can hear him.

PIPPA. He's with the other lot, isn't he? How on earth can you be friends?

BILL. We agree on the fundamentals.

PIPPA. Fundamentals?

BILL. Europe!

PIPPA. Well, he'll probably have a better career with the
Tories. This bunch certainly won't be around much longer.

MRS L. Shhh! For goodness sake!

PIPPA. Quite apart from old Clem's lumbago –

MRS L. Please!

PIPPA. I don't care if the cripple hears me! – the Foreign Sec's
practically dead, and the Chancellor's completely bonkers,
isn't he?

MRS L. Shhhhhhhhh!

PIPPA. Stop shushing me, you witch. (*To* BILL.) Hold this.
I won't be a sec.

BILL (*desperate*). No, wait!

MRS L (*equally desperate, together with* BILL). Don't go
anywhere!

PIPPA. I have to!

   PIPPA *exits.*

MRS L. That's it. She's had her lot.

BILL. Mrs L, please. Please!

MRS L. I'm the manager of this office – I'll do what's right,
thank you. Any rate, the moment Mr Attlee makes a
complaint, it's out of my hands. You've fallen in love with
an idea of something there, Bill, if you don't mind my
saying.

BILL. In love?

MRS L. Can't you see what she's really like?

BILL. She's perfection.

MRS L. My arse. Shhh. Here he is.

   The PRIME MINISTER *enters, talking to someone, over his
   shoulder, offstage.*

   PIPPA *runs in from the other side, smoothing down her
   skirt, takes her folders from* BILL *and gets in line, just –
   just! – in time for the* PM *to turn round and see them all.*

ATTLEE. Right. What's the schedule?

MRS L. Briefing with Jean Monnet, sir, about the Schuman Plan.

ATTLEE. Ah yes. Come to have his knuckles rapped.

MRS L. Then the National Executive at eleven.

ATTLEE. What have we got on Korea?

PIPPA (*handing over a report*). Received at midnight.

ATTLEE (*reading*). When's the Ambassador due?

PIPPA. Requested a postponement.

ATTLEE. What's his name?

BILL (*sotto*). Kim Jin-pyo.

PIPPA. Kim Jin-pyo.

ATTLEE (*closing the folder*). Won't do. We need him in ASAP. Let me know the moment he arrives. I must see him before lunch.

PIPPA. Very good, sir. (*Exits.*)

ATTLEE. Now, to this blasted Frenchman. Let's have a look.

BILL *passes the relevant folder.*

. . . (*Reading at the same time.*) Hmm. Jean Monnet. Who's with me on this one?

MRS L. No one, sir. You remember, Mister Monnet requested a one-to-one, without aides?

ATTLEE. Why did we agree to that? We had dealings with him when he was Deputy Secretary General of the League of Nations, didn't we?

MRS L. Yes, sir.

ATTLEE. He's arrived?

MRS L. Yes.

ATTLEE. A *fonctionnaire*, for God's sake. An international palm-presser; an elbow-squeezer with a large address book. (*Shaking his head at the notes.*) We spend far too much time rescuing these damned Europeans from one self-inflicted disaster after another. (*Looking up at* BILL.) What do you make of it?

BILL (*surprised*). Me, sir?

ATTLEE. I know your true colours. Do you see anything in this plan? Anything good, I mean.

BILL. Absolutely. I think we should jump in with both feet.

ATTLEE *laughs.*

. . . In my opinion, it's a first step along a path that could actually lead to permanent peace in Europe. It might even be the beginning of a movement away from old forms of nationalism, even of state government.

ATTLEE. Oh, good-oh! Got the Treasury report on it?

BILL *hands over another folder.*

. . . (*Again, speaking and reading at the same time.*) I can't decide whether it's a Catholic conspiracy or a German one. If it's another attempt at Federalism, it'll be Catholic. Every major European government except this one's run by religious fanatics and sponsored by the Church. Nothing'll stop the buggers till they've created a new Holy Roman Empire from the Atlantic shores of Portugal to the borders of Soviet Russia. Close your mouth, Bill.

BILL (*who's gaping in horror at what he hears*). Sorry, sir. I'm sure it's not a conspiracy of any sort.

ATTLEE. Bring him in.

BILL. Right you are, sir.

ATTLEE. Apologise for keeping him waiting, and, Bill, stay with us, will you?

BILL (*amazed*). Really?

ATTLEE. Yes, he can't object to you, you're not senior enough.

BILL (*delighted*). Absolutely, sir.

ATTLEE. And perhaps you can make some sense of it.

BILL. Sir! (*Exits.*)

ATTLEE. If I ever want to know what to think about something, Mrs L, I ask that young man his opinion and then I take the opposite view.

MRS L. You'd have thought the war would have knocked some of that silliness out of him.

ATTLEE. I don't know where Personnel get them.

MRS L. Tea, sir?

ATTLEE. No, it won't take long enough for tea. You know what this is? It's classic French expediency. German industry's getting back on its feet, and the French can't bear it. They start haranguing Germany, and the tit for tat starts all over again. So the Americans weigh in, pressurising the French to stop. Last thing they want's another European war. The French need to save face and find a way out. Monsieur Monnet hatches a plan with what looks to me, by the way, like a thinly veiled federalist plot. Schuman sees it as his chance to get the Americans off his back, and then with no warning whatsoever announces it as a bloody *fait accompli* on French radio. As if they actually intend to go ahead with it! And now I have to give the bloody civil servant –

MONNET *and* BILL *enter.*

. . . (*Smoothly.*) My dear Jean, how are you?

MONNET. Prime Minister.

MONNET *is a huge force, tactical and brilliant. Here, anticipating cynicism and obstruction, he is concerned to keep his emotions in check. He speaks with a slight accent.*

ATTLEE. Come in. Sit down.

MRS L *exits.* ATTLEE, MONNET *and* BILL *move to a separate part of the stage where there are two comfortable chairs and an upright, set out for a meeting.*

. . . (*Introducing and explaining* BILL.) You don't mind? Bretherton. He's not departmental.

MONNET *goes to object but* ATTLEE *continues.*

. . . Now then, I don't have long. If the Koreans arrive, I'll have to leave you.

MONNET. Of course.

*BILL sits between the other two men, on the upright, and prepares to take minutes. He excitedly cracks open a fresh new notepad.*

ATTLEE. I simply don't understand how this can have happened. We told the *Quai D'Orsay* if they want to make any announcement that affects Germany they're to pass it through me first.

MONNET. I apologise sincerely, Prime Minister, if the timing caused you any embarrassment.

ATTLEE (*bristling*). Embarrassment? It's just that it's hard to imagine how we can go back on it now it's been said.

MONNET. We don't want to go back on it.

ATTLEE. But . . . You don't? But surely –

MONNET. You think we were joking?

ATTLEE. As I understand it, your plan proposes you and Germany pool your coal and steel resources –

MONNET. It is the French Foreign Minister's, Monsieur Schuman's plan.

ATTLEE. I am quite aware whose plan it is.

MONNET. I am the architect. The French Foreign Minister is the sponsor.

ATTLEE (*irritably*). I really don't care.

MONNET. But I think it's important to understand that the plan has the entire backing of the Foreign Minister –

ATTLEE. Yes, and why has Schuman got involved? Because France got its wrists slapped by the Americans. The first sign of new growth in German heavy industry and France starts acting up –

MONNET. Precisely. And the plan addresses this point exactly.

ATTLEE. Well, go on then. Explain it to me.

MONNET. I intend to.

ATTLEE. I understand what you're aiming for but I can't for the life of me see how it could work.

MONNET. The outcome of both European wars this century has been decided purely and simply by one factor. Neither national merit nor personal bravery. Simply by whose industrial system can deliver the shells to the front with most efficiency. But if no one were to own the industry . . .

ATTLEE *is staggered.*

ATTLEE. What do you mean 'no one were to own it'? Someone will own it.

MONNET. We want to tie France and Germany so tightly together in a mutual embrace, if you catch my meaning, that neither can pull away far enough to hit the other one.

ATTLEE. You haven't answered the question. Who would own the industry?

MONNET. There would be a High Authority.

ATTLEE. Controlled by you?

MONNET. Me?

ATTLEE. France.

MONNET. No.

ATTLEE. Well, it certainly wouldn't be controlled by Germany! We only gave them back the right of self-government in the spring.

MONNET. No. It is autonomous. It is above.

ATTLEE. Can you explain what that means?

MONNET. The scheme involves an amount of sinking of national interests into a supranational body –

ATTLEE. How would it be elected?

MONNET. French and German citizens, experts in their field, would run it, but their role would transcend nation. They would, in effect, be the functionaries of a new community.

ATTLEE. It wouldn't be democratically elected then?

MONNET. Not in the sense that you mean, no.

ATTLEE. What other sense is there?

BILL *is so caught up in the argument that his notes slide off his knees.*

MONNET. I have come here today to ask you, Prime Minister, what chance is there that Britain will join in the plan?

ATTLEE (*aghast*). I rather thought that you had come here today so that I could haul you over the coals for announcing this sch– . . . Britain join in?!

MONNET. Italy, Belgium, Holland and Luxembourg have all expressed their willingness to join their industries to those of France and Germany. They see the opportunities that this plan affords.

ATTLEE. I'm sure they do. But what on earth has it got to do with us? Do you imagine I would want to tie the United Kingdom to a living corpse?

MONNET. Sir, if you fear losing influence by working together with other nations, rather than simply dictating terms, how do you think a country like . . . Luxembourg faces this dilemma?

ATTLEE (*laughing*). Perhaps it makes sense for the dear old Duchy of Luxembourg. The minnows of Europe have always needed the protection of a bigger neighbour. But I really can't imagine any *serious* country engaging –

PIPPA *enters.* BILL *stands.*

. . . What is it?

PIPPA. Our man in Korea, sir, on the telephone.

ATTLEE. Excuse me, gentlemen.

ATTLEE *exits with* PIPPA, *leaving* BILL *alone with* MONNET.

BILL *is beside himself with excitement.* MONNET *is frustrated about being abandoned.*

BILL. Voudriez-vous quelque chose a boire? Du thé? [Is there anything I can get you to drink? Tea?]

MONNET (*indicating that he is flattered by the use of French*). Non, merci. [No, thank you.] And do not think of offering me your coffee.

MONNET *gets up and irritably wanders about. After a while,* BILL *summons the courage to speak.*

BILL. Sir, I –

MONNET (*about the painting of the King*). Extraordinary the resemblance, don't you think?

BILL. To whom?

MONNET. Kaiser Wilhelm. A real Hohenzollern face.

ATTLEE *re-enters.*

. . . What news, Prime Minister?

ATTLEE. If the North doesn't invade the South within the week it'll be a miracle. (*Opening the Treasury folder.*) Now, the Treasury boys tell me that, according to their calculations, for a while, British steel could hold its own outside the plan, but eventually you could attack our exports and probably even our domestic markets.

MONNET. I see. So you are making a case to join the scheme?

ATTLEE. No, I am making a case to destroy the scheme.

MONNET. But if you will engage with these issues only from a detailed fiscal point of view –

ATTLEE. I don't regard the jobs of the 1.2 million British men who are engaged in the coal and steel industries as 'detail'. Or is there more to your scheme than you're letting on? Of course! That's right! The political implications. What do you say, Jean? Is political federation an essential prerequisite for your plan to work?

MONNET. Not necessarily. Not yet, at any rate.

ATTLEE. But it's what you're aiming for eventually.

BILL (*who can bear it no longer*). Yes! (*And then immediately.*) Sorry, sir.

ATTLEE. Is he right?

MONNET. There would be political implications, but federation is a long way off.

ATTLEE. You see! You bloody federalists. You're all the same. You speak in commerce but you think in politics.

BILL, *working hard to cover up his horror at this rudeness, manically fiddles with his pen top.* MONNET *swallows the insult.*

MONNET. I do not speak in commercial terms. You are the person who reads Treasury figures to me. Sir, attempt to rise above the mercantile. There is more to life than prudent economics.

ATTLEE. And so we should hand over to some supranational authority, staffed by Frenchmen and Germans, the right to close down our pits and steelworks, and perhaps turn over large sections of our populace to unemployment? No. That's the national government's prerogative!

MONNET. So it is the political implications of the plan you object to?

ATTLEE. Only because you pretend there are none.

MONNET. I am hiding nothing.

BILL *continues to fiddle with his pen, bursting to speak, but dares not.* PIPPA *enters.* BILL *stands.* PIPPA *approaches* ATTLEE *as before, but he stops her.*

ATTLEE (*to* PIPPA). Wait a moment.

MONNET. There is an open federalist debate raging in Europe that has not even begun here –

ATTLEE. People aren't interested –

BILL (*emboldened by* PIPPA's *presence*). Because they're not educated! If they only knew . . . Sorry, sir.

MONNET. Speak up, young man! If you are on my side, I need your support.

BILL (*contrite*). I'm sorry. I shouldn't say anything – it's not my place.

ATTLEE. No, go on. Give the argument some balance, Bill.

BILL. May I really speak openly, sir?

ATTLEE. But not naively, if at all possible.

BILL (*intensely aware of* PIPPA's *gaze, as well as* MONNET's *potential approval*). I believe it is vital that the full scope of this plan is not withheld from the people of this country. They only think nationalistically out of habit and ignorance. If the plan and its implications were explained to them, they would understand and embrace it. I'm sure about that.

MONNET. Ah, this young man has insight!

BILL. The vital importance of the plan should not be underestimated.

MONNET. You need to listen to the people of his generation, Prime Minister.

BILL (*gesturing to* MONNET). I, I, I, I . . . Well, the humiliation of the French at a point when they are prepared to act *altruistically* towards their old enemy would be a mistake of tragic proportions.

MONNET. Bravo.

BILL (*to* ATTLEE). I'm sorry, sir, I –

ATTLEE. But I simply don't see anything altruistic in it.

BILL (*now a little carried away*). And if the plan falters without us, we might be blamed.

ATTLEE. Or thanked.

BILL. And, purely practically, getting in at this stage we'd have more power to shape it.

ATTLEE. Alright, Bill, that's enough! (*Turning to* PIPPA.) What is it?

PIPPA. The National Executive is here, sir.

ATTLEE. Alright.

PIPPA *exits.*

MONNET. These constant interruptions, Prime Minister! What we are talking about here is of immense international significance –

ATTLEE (*angry*). Quite so. The Koreans, the Americans and the National Executive must wait while we discuss your airy-fairy federalist claptrap. Altruistic? No. Your foreign policy is governed entirely by fear of a resurgent Germany –

MONNET. Is that ignoble? English foreign policy is governed entirely by fear of another Armada –

ATTLEE. Absolutely. And what your plan proposes would wipe out everything we've gained in two world wars. For French fear of losing sovereign power, we must sacrifice some of our own? No. Not with a parliamentary majority of three. We are an island of coal, surrounded by fish. None of it is negotiable. Now, I must attend to the Executive –

MONNET. Only three seats, yes. And Winston understands the necessity of federation. He urges the creation of the United States of Europe.

ATTLEE. Only while he's out of power. Currently, he is painting and sketching in Marrakech as far as I know, and I am the Prime Minister. When the old man talks of the United States of Europe he doesn't imagine Britain *in* it! *Running* it maybe, or sitting by, making encouraging noises. If this country is allied with anyone, it's with the Commonwealth and what's left of the Empire, not with you Europeans.

MONNET. Are *you* not Europeans?

ATTLEE. We have full employment as our avowed aim. France, Germany, Italy, Holland . . . They're all run by Catholic anti-Socialist parties.

MONNET. Did you say Catholic? What is the significance that they are Catholic?

ATTLEE. Well, who *is* behind it? Germany?

MONNET. No one is 'behind it'. This is paranoia!

ATTLEE. The main supporters of the plan are yourself, Schuman, de Gasperi and Chancellor Adenauer. That's a Germanic alliance, culturally speaking.

MONNET. This is preposterous.

ATTLEE. Believe me, I'm mild in my response. If the Foreign Secretary were here, he'd be screaming 'Betrayal' at our even discussing the possibility of an alliance of any sort with Germany. (*Warming to his task.*) Let's see. The Italian President, de Gasperi, is a German speaker, isn't he? He might be running Italy now but in the last days of the Austro-Hungarian Empire, he was a pro-German politician in charge of Vienna. Right? The German Chancellor hates the British since an English brigadier ousted him as the Mayor of Cologne in the war and banished him to the countryside. And he speaks absolutely no English! Schuman might be the French Foreign Secretary but German's his first language. Actually, let's not beat about the bush. The French Foreign Secretary's a German, isn't he?

MONNET (*only just keeping his rage in check*). You use the fact that Monsieur Schuman is German to discredit the plan? He is not German. Luxembourg may be a country of no significance to you, but Monsieur Schuman was born there. The German Chancellor doesn't speak English? Does the Prime Minister speak German?

ATTLEE. Now, take care, Jean.

MONNET. Well, do you?

ATTLEE. No, I don't!

MONNET. Precisely. But the German people do not see this as a conspiracy against them! The Italian President is Austrian. Yes! Good! Why not? And to you I am French. '*You*,' he says to me, when he means '*France*'. '*Your* foreign policy' when he means 'French foreign policy'. I do not speak for France. I am not French. I am not German. Sir, I am European! This determination to assign us all to our little nationalities will no longer work. People who grew up in Saarland, Lorraine, Alsace are neither French nor German, or they are both. Fighting in the German army in the First World War and then for the French Army in the Second, because the land had reverted to France. Murdering their neighbours and those they grew up with. Where I come from, on the mantelpieces they have the Legions D'honneurs alongside the Iron Cross. Monuments to French and German dead in the same town squares. (*He is too moved to continue easily.*) Please let us not continue to sit around, awarding black marks to countries for bad behaviour, like school children playing war games. Let us, now we have finally crawled broken and bitter into the second half of the twentieth century, grow up a little, put behind us the old concepts. Prime Minister, this is not about who is, at the moment, 'top dog', as you would say. This is an exercise in collaboration, in which countries will relinquish some of the old aspirations, aspirations that have kept the endless competition for 'top dog' alive.

BILL, *just preventing himself from spontaneously clapping the last speech, nods and takes notes passionately.*

ATTLEE *takes a deep breath and sighs. He rises, stiff with lumbago. There is a pause.*

ATTLEE. That's enough. The meeting's over, gentlemen. I think this room needs some air through it. I'll meet the National Executive upstairs. I'd better have a quick look at the notes before I go up. (*Noticing that* MONNET *seems incapable of moving.*) Goodbye, sir.

BILL *gives* ATTLEE *another folder.*

MONNET. It is over?

ATTLEE (*to* MONNET, *while simultaneously reading from the folder*). You know, I'd be more impressed with your request for us to join your scheme if I actually believed you meant it.

BILL (*without thinking*). What?!

ATTLEE (*to* BILL). You think he means it?

BILL. Of course he means it.

ATTLEE. Really? Is Monsieur Monnet not playing with us?

BILL, *aghast, looks to* MONNET *for a contradiction.*

MONNET. It is immaterial what I want. You have excluded yourselves. You will wait and see first how the thing functions. You always do.

ATTLEE. Sounds like eminent sense to me.

MONNET (*becoming stonier*). But maybe it will be too late. The happy picture of Britain leading Europe cannot last for ever. The time will come when you will need us. Perhaps then you will find it hard to persuade us that you are sufficiently European.

ATTLEE. Is that a threat?

MONNET. You obstruct the Council of Europe, so that it has no power. You destroyed the Customs Union in '48.

BILL (*to* MONNET, *incredulous*). So you don't want Britain to join in the plan?

MONNET (*with thunder in his voice*). I will not let you destroy yet another genuine Franco-German attempt at a solution to our own problem. The new authority will meet in Luxembourg. I will chair it. I will set the agenda.

ATTLEE. Who are you, sir, to dictate the future? You are not even in the French government. You are merely a civil servant! Good day to you. Bretherton will see you out. (*Exits.*)

MONNET (*shouting after* ATTLEE). I will welcome the participants to the Grand Duchy with the words, 'Gentlemen! You are the first Government of Europe.'

MONNET *gathers himself.*

. . . (*To* BILL.) I know the way, thank you.

MONNET *strides off in the opposite direction from the* PM, *leaving* BILL *alone onstage, dazed.* PIPPA *re-enters, and potters pointlessly round her desk while* BILL *clears up after the meeting.*

PIPPA. Blew poor Monsieur Monnet out of the water?

BILL (*to* PIPPA). The word 'federal' sent Clem into a panicking tailspin. It's going to take longer than we imagined.

PIPPA. At last he realises.

BILL. You're not surprised?

PIPPA. You're really rather stupid for such a clever person, aren't you? They may be socialists but they've still got an empire.

BILL. They're internationalists, aren't they, in their own way.

PIPPA. Keep dreaming, Bill.

BILL. They're a radical government. They've been radical in their approach to everything else.

PIPPA. But Europe's different altogether. A quantum leap too far, even for this lot. Anyway, they haven't been radical for a while now –

BILL. What about the others? Do you think they'd be any better?

PIPPA. Worse, I'd think.

BILL. But Churchill –

PIPPA. Some of them might get it, I suppose. Your friend Teddy does anyway. Their education sort of encourages them to flirt with the idea of a cosy kind of European togetherness, doesn't it? Well, at least they sometimes go there on holiday, speak a bit of French, know a bit of Italy.

BILL. Do you think I overstepped the mark with the PM?

PIPPA. What?

BILL. You said I should stand up for myself and I did.

PIPPA. Oh, sorry, Bill, I really wasn't listening.

BILL. Oh, what an appalling fiasco.

PIPPA (*picking up her handbag*). What are you talking about? I'm the one with the hellish hangover. (*Exits.*)

BILL *trots after* PIPPA *as the lights fade.*

## ACT TWO

### Scene One

*We return to the pebble beach in Aldston, Suffolk.*

*A projection reminds us that it's 1992.*

*It is late afternoon, the day after Act One, Scene Three, took place.*

*The wind has picked up. The sea is rough. It's bitterly cold.*

*The wood-hulled boat is still beached on the shingle.*

*We're aware of other boats too, because we hear the wind banging against rigging, metal and rope, and the creak and groan of boats in the water.*

*The ladder remains in place.*

*The lights come up on the two characters from the earlier scene, KEN and HILARY.*

*KEN seems even more defeated than he was in the previous scene, his rage barely contained.*

*With them is SELIMA. She is a journalist, underdressed for the wintry beach conditions. She has a notebook, a tape recorder (which is pretty ineffectual against the wind) and some bumph about KEN's boat and HILARY's campaign.*

*The light is fading fast. As the scene progresses, the sky will get darker until there is no daylight left. At the same time, a full moon will appear. And the arc light of a nearby lighthouse will sweep the stage with numbing regularity.*

HILARY. But I thought Townsend were coverin' this –

SELIMA. He was going to, but when you brought it forward at the last minute –

HILARY. MAFF brought it forward.

SELIMA. Still, he found himself double-booked.

HILARY. But Townsend knows all abowt it. 'E's been followin' my campaign fer months now.

SELIMA. It's the dog show tonight, you see. Mr Townsend's been committed to that for months.

HILARY. Christ! A load a tarted-up poodles bein' far more important 'an –

SELIMA. Of course not. Not more important.

HILARY. So we've got yoo.

SELIMA. Yes, you've got me.

HILARY. How long yoo been workin' fer the 'erald?

SELIMA. Long enough I imagine to –

HILARY. What do yoo know 'bowt this then?

SELIMA. Well, I've got the latest bumph you sent in, and I'm a very fast learner.

HILARY. What did yoo say yoor name were?

SELIMA. Selima. Selima Sakaria.

HILARY. Where's tha' from then?

SELIMA. It's Turkish.

HILARY. Is it? God almigh'y.

SELIMA. Is that a problem?

HILARY (*shaking her head*). Bloody Townsend. (*To SELIMA.*) This yoor first job, gal?

SELIMA. I don't see what that's –

HILARY. It is!

SELIMA. Listen, I've got a very good degree from the London School of Journalism –

HILARY. What the 'ell yoo dooin' 'ere then?

SELIMA. What?!

HILARY. Yoor from London –

SELIMA. Originally. My husband's from here.

HILARY. Well, if yoor the best they can come up with, I s'pose I gotta –

SELIMA. Look, for goodness sake, let's just get on with it, before I lose all the feeling in my hands, and I can't write anything.

KEN (*to* HILARY). I told yoo, gal, I ent 'avin' no newspapers! (*To* SELIMA.) Nothing personal. I jus' don't want no one else gettin' involved.

HILARY. Ken, 'er bein' 'ere ent gooin' a make no difference to yoo –

KEN. Is tha' right?

HILARY. But it'll make a big difference to the campaign –

KEN. So wha' I want ent of no importance –

HILARY. If we can get this in the papers, this could really change people's –

KEN. You are makin' this a hell of a lot harder, yoo know tha'?

KEN *puts his hands in his pockets and walks away.*

SELIMA, *undeterred, doggedly follows* KEN, *her journalistic instincts aroused.*

SELIMA. I understand what you're going through must be very tough, Ken –

KEN. I don't reckon yoo can doo.

SELIMA. No. But I'd like to get something of your point of view, if that's alright.

KEN. Not really, noo.

SELIMA. Just tell me . . . how do you feel about –

KEN. How the fuck do yoo think I feel?

SELIMA. Right.

HILARY (*to* SELIMA). He won't talk about the boot.

KEN (*to* HILARY). Don't yoo dare goo apologisin' fer me.

SELIMA (*undeterred by* KEN*'s rage*). This is it, is it? 'The Mearston'. And you share ownership of it with – (*Reading from bumph.*) a Mr MacLean?

KEN *doesn't answer.*

HILARY. Yeah, we do.

SELIMA. Why's he not here too, then?

HILARY. They built it t'gether, in '81. So it's only 'ad ten years fishin'. Got another thirty in it prob'ly. See, Ken thought Jason would 'ave it when 'e was owd enough –

SELIMA (*to* HILARY). Your son? Is he going to be a fisherman too, like his dad?

HILARY. If yoo'd read that, yoo'd know.

SELIMA. He's not interested then?

HILARY. 'E's interested! The point is . . . Christ alive!

SELIMA. Tell me.

HILARY. There won't be n'more fish'men in this family! Yoo understan' that?

KEN. My owd man set me up in me firs' boot. I thought I'd done the same fer Jason, buildin' this. (*His emotions get to him.*) Ent able. Noo way.

SELIMA. I see. I understand . . . They're interfering with your right to pass what you know on to your son . . .

KEN *looks at* SELIMA.

KEN (*to* HILARY). If she's staying, she'll need a stiffer jacket. There's one in the boot.

SELIMA. Oh, do you have something? I would really appreciate it.

HILARY *looks at* SELIMA *and* KEN *in disbelief, and climbs the ladder into the boat.*

. . . What happened to your hand?

KEN. Nuthin'. Got numb 'ands workin' the trawlers. Bandage it stop it snaggin', or puttin' it down on some'in 'ot an' not noticin'.

SELIMA. What are you going to do?

KEN (*sarcastically enthusiastic*). Oh, I got a mate wants me t'sell waterbeds with 'im, door to door. Or maybe I could go into sekoority or summin'.

SELIMA. Bloody hell.

KEN. You got it, gal.

SELIMA. It must mean a lot to you that Hilary's fighting so hard for –

KEN (*curtly*). Right. She's busy enough.

SELIMA *considers.*

SELIMA. Not helping you though, is it?

KEN *doesn't answer. She's got through to him. She puts a hand on* KEN*'s arm with genuine feeling and* KEN *doesn't move away.*

HILARY, *displeased, throws a windcheater down from the boat.*

. . . Oh, thank God.

KEN (*awkward, moving away a little*). Where's this monkey from the Ministry, then?

*The windcheater doesn't suit or fit Selima at all.*

SELIMA. That's great, Hilary.

HILARY (*climbing back down the ladder*). 'E's late, ent 'e.

SELIMA. Now this would be the man from (*Consulting the bumph.*) the Ministry of Farming and Fishing, right?

HILARY. Yeah, supervisin' the decommission.

SELIMA. How long's he going to be, then? 'Cause I've got to catch a bus soon, else I'll miss the last train that actually gets me home tonight.

HILARY. I'll give 'em a ring, make sure 'e's on 'is way.

KEN (*moving right away from the women, down towards the water*). We ent chasin' round after 'im. If 'e can't be bothered t'turn up . . .

SELIMA (*kicking her heels together to keep warm*). Now, tell me about your campaign, Hilary. Not many housewives go to Brussels and represent local business. How did it all start?

HILARY. Started one day when MAFF sent us the third load a new regoolations we'd 'ad in a month. These regoolations all come out of the EU, see.

SELIMA. EU? Is that what it's called now?

HILARY (*only just patiently*). Yeah, since Maastricht last year. Don't they let yoo read newspapers in journalist school?

SELIMA. Our readers aren't going to be interested in Europe and that sort of thing to be honest –

HILARY. Jesus! If someone whips a dog in Cleethorpes it's front-page national noos. They destroy an industry and yoo can't keep people's attention. It's Europe. It's borin'.

SELIMA. It's sub-zero. That's the trouble.

HILARY. Billions a pounds on our tax goo to Brussels every year. Why ent people int'rested?

SELIMA. No, what I'm beginning to understand is that this campaign's really taken on a life of its own –

HILARY. See, yoo got to get across how makin' a livin' in this industry's borderline at the best a times, an' then –

SELIMA. And, to be honest, Hilary, you seem well . . . exhausted. How has running the campaign affected things between you and Ken?

HILARY (*angrily*). Listen, yoo asked 'ow the campaign started. I'm tellin' yoo. This one month we got three separate packages! Ken was sayin' 'e was givin' up. 'E was gooin' a chuck it in and do away with 'imself. That personal enough for you?

SELIMA. Yeah, that's much better.

HILARY. An' it ent jus' fishin'. It's the same all over. Farmers, small business, 'ooever you talk to.

SELIMA. And then the campaign gained momentum when Ken decided to accept the decommission package. Did it surprise you? Him agreeing to decommission the boat, I mean.

HILARY. 'E's a fish'man. That ent a job yoo jus' give up.

SELIMA. But he was desperate.

HILARY. An' 'e's not the only one. Tha's wha' I'm sayin'. Derek, up near Butley Creek. 'E's on the phone to Ken. Cryin' 'e was. 'Onest a God. Great big man, and 'e's crying

down the phone. Been stopped on his way to market to sell
his sheep. MAFF inspectors're tellin' 'im there's a new
European regoolation says 'e's got to get a tachograph put
in 'is Land Rover –

SELIMA. What on earth's a tachograph?

HILARY. It's one a them spy-in-the-cab things, make sure yoo
take enough breaks. Regoolation's only meant for them
great juggernauts that stuff up the motorways, not a four-ton
truck with a few sheep on a back lane. I mean, 'ow many
breaks do a sheep need? But in this country it's been
applied to everythin' above three an' an 'alf tons. So now
Derek's gotta spend seven hundred quid to fit a tachograph.
'E's back against the wall as it is.

SELIMA*'s taking notes, but not about the tachograph.*

SELIMA. Yeah, right. So, were you disappointed in Ken's
decision to give up fishing?

HILARY. I got loads more stuff typed up at 'ome; other cases
just as barmy.

SELIMA. I mean the future's very uncertain for you both now.
How disappointed were you?

HILARY. I thought 'e'd look 'arder for another way owt
maybe.

SELIMA. Uh-huh.

HILARY. 'E's always been more of a fish'man than an
'usband, if yoo know wha' I mean. On our 'oneymoon 'e
spent more time fishin' for 'erring off the pier than 'e did
with me. Two poles, a buoy made from a washin'-up bottle
'e got out the dustbins at the back a the hotel, an' a Wimpy
for bait.

HILARY *suddenly stops, her emotions having caught her
out.* SELIMA *lets the silence last.*

KEN *is looking out to sea.*

KEN (*to* SELIMA). 'Ere.

SELIMA *approaches* KEN.

. . . Yoo see the lights ow' there? 'Bowt three, four mile owt.

SELIMA. Erm. Yeah, yeah.

KEN. It's one a them foreign factory trawlers that work our waters. The EU gives 'em licenses to do it. Trawl so wide yoo could put a jumbo jet in it.

SELIMA *snorts.*

HILARY. No. Literally. A jumbo jet. They catch more in a day 'an this boot could land in a year.

SELIMA. But hang on. I don't understand. Isn't there an international limit or something? Two hundred miles, isn't it?

HILARY. Tha's changed.

SELIMA. What do you mean?

HILARY. These seas ent ours n'more. Any EU country's allowed t' fish 'ere now. Tha' out there, tha's not the North Sea. It's a common European resource.

SELIMA. I had no idea.

HILARY. Decommissionin's the only way we could possibly pay the fine.

SELIMA. The fine?

HILARY. That Ken and MacLean got for overfishin'.

SELIMA. What did they do wrong?

KEN. Broke the law.

SELIMA (*about the bumph*). Is that in here?

HILARY. It ent that simple.

SELIMA. Well, they either broke the law or they didn't.

KEN. Listen, you can make a profit off a small boat like this, 'cause a the quotas, and the company trawlers are docked two hundred days a year 'cause a the restrictions.

HILARY. What 'appened was they was landin' the catch just 'ere, where we're standin'. Five MAFF officials pile out on cars up there, an' come runnin' 'cross the beach like storm troopers.

SELIMA. They must have overfished one hell of a lot.

KEN. Exceeded our monthly quota on cod by 300lbs.

SELIMA. Doesn't sound like much.

HILARY. It ent. N'more 'an a hundred fish.

> KEN *again walks away, this time to the boat.*

SELIMA. So the man from MAFF is coming to collect the fine.

HILARY. No, 'e's comin' to decommission the boot. Yoo end up with no boot and no money, but there ent no choice. Look, I reckon this story could be much bigger 'an the Ipswich 'erald, if you get it righ'.

> SELIMA *notices* KEN, *who is leaning on his boat, head bowed, and* HILARY *follows her gaze.*

> . . . (*Approaching* KEN.) Come on, love, we'll get throo this.

> KEN *pulls sharply away from* HILARY. *He turns to* SELIMA. *He speaks calmly but there's a seething anger underneath.*

KEN. I reckon it's what the gov'ment wants, see. No boots dooin' no fishin'.

SELIMA. Ok, I think I've got what I need.

HILARY. No, I want yoo to get photographs on it.

SELIMA. Of what?

HILARY. The destruction.

SELIMA. What of?

HILARY. We 'ad an offer on it from the Conservation Society in Great Yarmouth, an' all. They wanted it for their museum. But you don't get yoor money till the boot's demolished.

SELIMA. You're kidding me.

HILARY. It's not in the EU directive. Some brown suit at MAFF's jus' made it up and stuck it in. This is what they do. Turn a two-page guideline from Brussels into a thirty-

five-page list a restrictions an' apply it across the board.
Like we need more rools to live by. See, we ent no good at
this European thing. Other countries ignore what doesn't
suit 'em. We go and make it worse. Now, if you could get a
picture of –

SELIMA. What are they going to do? Take axes to it, or what?

HILARY. If yoo could get a picture on it in the paper, that
would show people what they're prepared t'do to the
industry –

SELIMA. But it'll take all night! How the hell are they going
to . . . ? Blow it up? This is crazy.

MACLEAN *enters, out of breath and furious, and makes
straight for* KEN.

MACLEAN. They ent gooin' a destroy it.

SELIMA. What?

MACLEAN. Wha' the bloody 'ell is gooin' on 'ere?

KEN. Listen, MacLean –

MACLEAN. Yoo weren't gooin' a tell me? Last I heard, we
'ad till Friday to make a decision.

KEN. We got a £147,000 fine. That's more 'an we earned since
we built 'er.

MACLEAN. There's a MAFF man in The Leg a Mutton 'bowt
to set off to do a bit a Ministry work. Thought it might have
somethin' to do wi' us.

KEN. Tell me, MacLean. 'Ow the flamin' 'ell else am I gooin'
a pay off seventy-three grand? 'Ow are yoo?

SELIMA. Wait a sec. I just need to know. You *are* going to
have your boat destroyed tonight, aren't you? Because if
nothing's happening, I've got a bus to catch.

MACLEAN. No we bloody ent.

KEN. Ah, yes; yool 'ave yoor entertainment.

SELIMA. Well, which is it?

KEN. It's gotta be done.

MACLEAN. No way, Ken. This boot's mine jus' as much as it's yoors, an' I say no way, boy!

*Lights change.*

## Scene Two

*The Prime Minister's private quarters, 10 Downing Street.*

*1972 is projected onto the set.*

*There is an oil painting of Queen Elizabeth II, and a clavichord.*

TEDDY, *now Prime Minister, is talking on the phone to the Norwegian Prime Minister.*

BILL, *now 46, and the PM's Private Secretary, is listening, concerned and attentive.*

*There is a separate small space on the stage, with a phone, a desk and possibly a photograph of a North Sea oil rig, that the Prime Minister of Norway, TRYGVE BRATTELI, will occupy for the conversation at the beginning of the scene.*

*It is early evening.*

TRYGVE. It will not work, Ted! I will lose everything! The opposition is –

TEDDY (*smoothly*). My dear Trygve, please remain calm.

TRYGVE. They have made a trap for us. I understand, as potential accession states, we must accept wholesale this expensive French agriculture package. But now this new fish policy? No. It is a deal breaker.

TEDDY. It's unfortunate. But it's vital we remember, you and I, that our job as leaders of our countries is to –

TRYGVE. But Ted! Suddenly now after months of careful negotiation they intend to rush this through at the last minute with no debate, and hope we will not notice? Of the four of us, Ireland and Denmark have huge fish supplies, but you have more. And if anyone knows anything about my country, it is that we have much fish! Between us we have nearly all the fish in Europe. 80%. But our Common Market friends may not share these resources without we accept this new fishing policy. Now, the lawyers here say it has no legal foundation. There is nothing in the treaties which permits it. Yet Brussels insists to push it through. It is serious stupidity if the original six only now realise they will take all four countries into their Common Market club and not have our fish. I think it is why they want Norway in the first place! Ted, we will challenge it together, yes?

TEDDY. I'm not sure that's the wisest path, Trygve.

TRYGVE. But it is illegal! What do your fishermen say?

TEDDY. I've no idea. I've not asked them. We're immensely frustrated, of course. But being at the mercy of this kind of sharp practice is the price we pay for not getting in at the beginning.

TRYGVE. Norway was not asked at the beginning.

TEDDY (*to* BILL). Get my suit, would you, Bill? Good chap.

BILL, *as concerned about the new development as* TRYGVE, *exits.*

TRYGVE. How can you even consider accepting it?

TEDDY (*into phone*). We must accept it. Denmark and Ireland will follow, and we're in!

TRYGVE. My Fishing Minister says he will resign. I fear the same sort of violent protests against the negotiation that brought down the government last year. Once news of it is out, we will for sure lose the referendum. Then *I* will have to go.

TEDDY (*the first sign of being in the least ruffled*). It is absolutely essential that the details of this fishing deal do *not* get out! There must be no questions about this!

TRYGVE. But they say they must have a decision tonight. I must consult –

TEDDY. No consultation, Trygve! Do you understand? I must have . . . opaqueness . . . before I get this through Parliament. I need your total support. Else we're all sunk.

BILL *returns with* TEDDY's *white tie and tails.*

. . . (*To* BILL.) Put it there.

TRYGVE. But I walk out of my office and I talk to the people on the street –

TEDDY. For God's sake, listen to me. When you talk to your people, concentrate on your successes, your derogations.

TRYGVE. We in Norway are asked to give away our fish! I cannot keep that from them. We are a sea people. Fish and ships.

TEDDY (*at first confused*). Oh! Ships! Yes. (*To* BILL.) And the score. The Elgar.

BILL *exits.*

. . . (*Into phone.*) This is the moment we've been waiting for, for a decade, Trygve. I have served tirelessly on accession talks under two previous British Prime Ministers. Scuttling backwards and forwards to Brussels, buried day and night in detailed negotiations about bauxite and butter, keeping infinitely long lists and a vast mass of detail in my head. And twice de Gaulle vetoed our efforts at the very last minute. Perhaps we really weren't European enough. Perhaps he knew we'd scupper his precious agricultural policy if we were in there, throwing our weight around. But now, I am in charge – and de Gaulle has gone. Trygve, there's an invisible hand that guides us into the right job at the right time. I believe taking my country into the Common Market is the job I was put on the earth to do.

TRYGVE. Being involved with Europe has never done us many favours. We remember the war –

TEDDY. You want to be left out in the cold with . . . I don't know . . . Lichtenstein?

TRYGVE. You urge – was the word 'opaqueness'? We have transparency. We call it democracy. (*After leaving a pause for effect.*) And we have oil. (*Another little effective pause.*) We do not have to join.

TEDDY. It is your destiny, as it is ours. To take part in a great joint venture –

TRYGVE. Oj, oj, oj, Ted, please . . .

TEDDY. . . . The construction of a European group of nations determined to reconcile the safeguarding of their national identities –

TRYGVE. Don't give me this bullshit –

TEDDY. I believe it, Trygve. I said it in Parliament. Joining the Community entails no loss of essential national sovereignty.

TRYGVE. No, just a loss of fish. Anyway, it rather depends on what you mean by 'essential'.

TEDDY. Of course we lose some sovereignty. That's the point. That's the deal. We relinquish sovereignty to the extent that we gain prosperity.

TRYGVE. Stop quoting from the brochure, Ted. I have a consultative role with the Norwegian people –

TEDDY. They won't ever understand the procedures involved in the transfer of power from –

TRYGVE. They will understand it if I explain it!

TEDDY. Then *don't explain it*!! Don't say anything! Don't have a referendum! Then you won't lose it!

BILL *returns with a large conductor's score and baton case.*

TRYGVE. The people will in time discover the true nature of this European enterprise, Ted, and I warn you, they will not forgive you then if you hide it from them now.

TEDDY. I don't suppose I shall be here then.

TRYGVE. The way things are going, I don't suppose I shall be here tomorrow!

TEDDY. Don't despair, Trygve. Perhaps we can negotiate an opt-out from the policy.

TRYGVE. An opt-out? A derogation you mean? No, that won't appease anyone.

TEDDY. The full impact would be delayed –

TRYGVE. But a derogation is merely a temporary exemption. It'll only delay the inevitable. Brussels will impose the fishing deal on us eventually.

TEDDY. Don't discount it. It's a useful trick.

TRYGVE. No, no, no. I will talk to my people. Goodnight, Ted.

TRYGVE *exits.*

TEDDY (*to* BILL). Honestly, he *will* keep talking to his people. I don't know how he ever gets anything done. Maybe Norwegians are different, but the British have no idea how their democracy works. I wouldn't dream of beginning to explain to them how their Bill of Rights'll be superseded by European law when Britain joins –

BILL (*interrupting sharply*). How long could we negotiate an opt-out for?

TEDDY (*taken aback by* BILL*'s direct tone*). I don't know, Bill. A decade?

BILL. So, by 1982, foreign boats'll be fishing up to six miles off our shore?

TEDDY. Possibly three miles. Now then, forgive me. I'm preoccupied. I must prepare for this orchestral performance. Of course the blasted TV cameras have to be there to record it. Help me into this, would you?

*Through the following,* BILL *helps* TEDDY *change into his white tie and tails.*

BILL (*taking* TEDDY*'s jacket from him*). Are you really intending to keep it hidden from the people?

TEDDY. Now I need quiet, Bill.

BILL. Won't there be questions in Parliament?

TEDDY (*unused to his wishes being ignored*). There are always means of avoiding questions. You ought to be congratulating me for getting us this far.

BILL. Should we not investigate the legality of it at least?

TEDDY. Is everything alright?

BILL. I phoned the Ministry. There's twenty-two thousand fishermen in Britain.

TEDDY. Twenty-two thousand, uneducated, rural, geographically dispersed fishermen. Won't be a problem. Anyway, nothing'll change for a while.

BILL (*taking* TEDDY's *trousers*). If you can get the derogation.

TEDDY. We'll give way on New Zealand rubber or ceramics or something. Eric or Geoff'll pull it off. Eric's been positively invaluable in Brussels. He can lip-read in three languages, you know –

BILL. But when it expires –

TEDDY. Actually, I'd love to have our usual chat this evening, but I must calm my mind for the performance.

BILL. Very well.

BILL, *silently frustrated, continues to dress* TEDDY.

TEDDY. I'm beginning to regret choosing the Overture 'Cockayne'. It's very difficult and no one knows it. And frankly the Festival Hall is a little daunting –

BILL (*propelled to speak*). Teddy, I'm sorry, but we've been friends for many years now. I've been by your side, with Geoffrey and Eric, night and day for many months. I think I've earned the right to say what's on my mind –

TEDDY. For goodness sake then, Bill, say it.

BILL. You mustn't accept this fishing deal.

TEDDY. That's ridiculous. Anyway, it's a non-negotiable. With European law you can never renegotiate. Look, we'll be allowed to fish in their waters. They're allowed to fish in ours. Our fisheries are dying anyway. We're going to have to swallow it.

TEDDY *is now fully dressed.*

. . . And compared to what we lose, we gain access to the whole continent. An enormous Free Trade Area.

BILL. Well, we already had one of those.

TEDDY. You're not defending the Commonwealth? You of all people. You're still on my side, aren't you, Bill?

BILL. Of course, but –

TEDDY. Enough of this sentimentality about the damned Commonwealth. It's really saying 'Empire', and the time is well overdue when we must just let that go. What the hell have we got to do with Botswana? No. Broadstairs! From the room where I was born, you could see the Belgian coast. It's a very narrow channel, kept wide by prejudice that's so old we don't know why we feel it. (*A sudden memory.*) Oh, I remember! Your people were fishermen.

BILL. Still are.

TEDDY. Ah, I understand. I forget, since you don't sound like one any more. Now let me see the score.

BILL *passes* TEDDY *the score.* TEDDY *flicks through it and plays small sections on the clavichord.*

BILL. I'm sorry to take your time. But I say this is too high a price to pay.

TEDDY. The price is immaterial.

BILL. I see.

TEDDY (*a well-oiled argument*). The important thing is that as soon as we're in, we can start to work with these countries and help determine the –

BILL. And you're seriously prepared to sacrifice the livelihood of – ?

TEDDY (*finally snapping, incensed*). Do you have any idea what I've achieved? No other Prime Minister has come close to engineering the psychic change necessary to get Parliament to engage seriously with Europe. No one had the balls till I came along! Macmillan – hopelessly fey about the whole thing. The conviction of a mouse. Let de Gaulle bully him mercilessly. His old friend. I never understood . . . And Wilson? Even worse. He never got it. Doesn't even know where Europe is. For Christ's sake, I was in Poland the day before war broke out. While you and I were fighting in Belgium and Holland, he was in Dundee, counting cheese for the Board of Trade.

BILL. You always say that. It was the Ministry of Food. And he was controlling potatoes.

TEDDY. But I! I have lion-tamed irreconcilables! On the one hand: avoid scaring the British public to death, not to mention the Commonwealth, by giving away too much too soon. On the other: avoid asking the EEC for special treatment all the time in order not to confirm their doubts about our seriousness. No one else has ever come close to this triumphant high-wire diplomacy. It's political aerobatics! Now, Bill, someone has to be able to see above the detail, and if there've been a few casualties along the way –

BILL. You make it sound like we're conceding next to nothing! It's who we are: coalminers, farmers and fishermen. Feelings about fishing run deeper than you can imagine. It's hunting. Ancient, prehistoric.

TEDDY. That's just nostalgia. This is what we've been waiting for all our lives, isn't it? Why would you baulk now? Deny the Common Market their meagre fishing rights and ruin the whole thing? Why would I fuck things up at the last hurdle?

BILL. Then I am not on your side any more.

TEDDY. You're still determined to be a fisherman's son. With the greatest respect to you, old friend, I haven't got time for this.

BILL. At least I know who I am. I don't think that's such a bad thing.

TEDDY (*feeling the barb*). I know who I am.

BILL. You've been wearing this immaculate . . . mask for so long, it is who you are.

TEDDY. Now listen to me. I can't afford to be stuck in the past, unable to see beyond the confines of this little island and its bloody fish. And since you insist on this conversation, I'll tell you something else that divides us. The truth is that you've only ever supported the idea of Integration –

BILL. Integration?

TEDDY. Because you're frightened of Nationalism.

BILL. Integration, Ted? You can't even say the word Federation any more.

TEDDY. I have no quarrel with Nationalism –

BILL. What?!

TEDDY. I am a patriot. I want us to be inside Europe as a means to secure our rightful place in the world.

BILL. Then it's you whose vision is limited to the confines of this little island.

TEDDY. Do you think we have any choice?! Sure, it was fine for Attlee to be high-handed. But we can't be choosy now. The economics have shifted. We're lagging behind the rest of Europe. We need Europe.

BILL. You're a patriot? You're a nationalist now?

TEDDY. What I am is the Prime Minister of this country.

TEDDY *stares at* BILL, *unflinchingly.*

BILL. I understand. You've indulged me enough.

TEDDY. You have picked a very bad night.

BILL (*one last attempt*). The Council has only given us till tonight to think about it.

TEDDY. I don't need more time. (*Pause.*) You can't understand because you're a civil servant and I'm a politician. I don't mean anything by that. It's just a statement of fact.

BILL. Right. I'll hand in my letter of resignation in the –

TEDDY. Bill, Bill, Bill. Not over fish.

BILL *is very upset and can't look at* TEDDY. TEDDY *is regretful, not for what he's said but for the rift that has been created between them.*

. . . I'm sorry it's come to this.

BILL. I don't suppose it'll have any impact on what you do. But I can't stand by and –

TEDDY. Quite right. Held your ground.

*The two men look at each other. They realise something irreversible has happened. Neither knows how to end the conversation with warmth, though both would like to. In the absence of either of them being able to make a definite move,* TEDDY *returns to where he feels safe.*

. . . If only Attlee'd gone in with the Schuman Plan, how easy it would have been. The way things were after the war, we'd be running the place now, dictating terms –

BILL, *who doesn't want to argue any more, just can't let this go.*

BILL (*wearily*). That isn't the point, though, is it? We're not in it to lead it.

TEDDY. Oh, bugger it, frankly, Bill. I can't be Communi – what's that bloody word?

BILL. *Communautaire.*

TEDDY (*appalling accent*). *Communau . . . Communau . . .* A good little European in my own bloody sitting room.

BILL. You've abandoned . . . everything, then.

TEDDY. There's one more thing you can do for me before you go.

BILL. What's that?

TEDDY. You've done this tie so tight I can barely breathe.

BILL *loosens the tie.*

Thanks. (*Turning to the score.*) Perhaps as a musical event it will not be one of the highest intelligence, but I hope the occasion will be magnificent. The music will carry us. So English and yet so universal. I witnessed for myself the power Elgar still exerts at the Last Night of the Proms this year. As I looked at that crowded hall, with thousands of people there, the promenade filled with young people, I heard them singing the great songs of our country. They stamped 'Rule, Britannia' and they sang 'Wider still and wider, shall thy bounds be set'. They sang it with passion because they believed it. They knew quite well that the world had moved on from the days of Empire. But they were crying out for a new advance down a different path. How can we satisfy the inner urge of those who were, that night, with such passion, singing the old words and wanting new meaning? The way will be hard and it will take time, but we can do it. And we must do it if we want to find a new forum for British leadership, if we want to find a new outlet for Britain's greatness!

BILL *exits.* TEDDY *turns to the audience as if it were the orchestra he is about to conduct.*

... Now then, ladies and gentlemen, if you're ready ...

TEDDY *raises his conductor's baton. The lights immediately go out. The auditorium is filled with Elgar.*

## Scene Three

*We return to the beach in Aldston. Almost no time has elapsed since the end of Act Two, Scene One.*

MACLEAN. 'Ow the 'ell did yoo think yoo was gooin' a get away wi' it?

KEN. It don't make no difference now, MacLean.

MACLEAN. It ent only up to yoo though, is it?

SELIMA. You're the joint owner, Mr MacLean?

MACLEAN (*to* SELIMA). There ent no story 'ere, gal. If yoo wanna story yoo should write about the gyppos. They steal our oil and they shit in the kiddies' playground. Nothin' 'appenin' 'ere. This boat ent bein' destroyed.

SELIMA (*to* KEN). Isn't it? Well, is it?

HILARY (*to* MACLEAN). There's no shiftin' 'im once 'e's made 'is mind up, MacLean, yoo know tha'.

MACLEAN. We made this boot together, yoo bastard.

SELIMA. Just give me a clue –

HILARY. Wait, for God's sake.

KEN. There ent no other way owt, MacLean. Why won't yoo face it?

MACLEAN (*to* HILARY). And yoor jus' lettin' this 'appen?

HILARY. Din't 'ave no choice, did we?

MACLEAN. An' good for yoor campaign too if they destroy the boot. Get yoo all this press attention.

HILARY. Wha' the 'ell are yoo talkin' 'bowt? The campaign's all 'bowt savin' the boot.

KEN. There ent no argument to be 'ad. We ent got the money for no argument.

MACLEAN. I'd rather kill meself than let 'em take –

KEN. You go an' kill yerself then; I ent stoppin' yer. There's a line wrapped rownd the drive shaft. That's a new line or a new drive shaft, or both. If I pay off the fine, I'm clear, I can leave things clear.

MACLEAN. It's some wimp from Ipswich, for Christ's sake. Why we takin' notice?

HILARY. Yoor livin' a dream world, MacLean. Yoo always were. 'E's gooin' a destroy the boot. It's the rools. Tha's why we're takin' notice.

MACLEAN. Tha's bollocks. We won't let 'im.

HILARY. What you gooin' a do? Shoot 'im?

MACLEAN (to KEN). We'll treat 'im like owd dut, boy. Tell 'im t'go stuff 'imself.

KEN. Yoo can pretend, but yoo and me ent partners n'more, MacLean.

MACLEAN (almost pleading). No, Ken, we'll go someplace else. We'll get a little shrimper, go up Lincolnshire. Yoo an' me owt there, talking bollocks an' catchin' fish.

KEN. 'Ow the 'ell yoo gooin' a chase anythin'? Yoo won't 'ave a boot!

MACLEAN. There's always a way.

KEN. But there ent the fish.

MACLEAN. They'll come back sometime, Ken, an' –

KEN. When did yoo last see an 'erring round 'ere, or a cod over four year? They're breedin' at diff'rent depths, in colder water, at diff'rent times a year –

MACLEAN. But if everyone chucks it in in the meantime, there'll be no fish'men with no knowledge when they do come back. It'll be a free-for-all between the Dutch an' the Spanish.

HILARY. Don't be stoopid. It already is.

KEN. Let's jus' take the money an' –

MACLEAN. It ent 'bowt the money! It's 'bowt the fishin! (*Definitively.*) I ent stoppin' fer no one, Ken. I ent gooin' a change. Neither should yoo. Yoor a religious nut on a fish'man. Yoo got a job as a deckie learner with Vincent's afore yoor seventeenth birthday. We was off Iceland afore we could drive.

KEN (*topping* MACLEAN). And last year we di'n't make a penny.

*This halts* MACLEAN *for a moment.*

. . . Tha's the truth, ent it.

MACLEAN *appears to be on the point of capitulating but then something like panic rises up inside him.*

MACLEAN. But if I can't do it, boy, what am I? I ent nuthin'.

KEN. Listen t' me. All I ever wanted was some place to go where there was no rools. No one tellin' me wha' to do an' 'ow t' do it. Me an' the openness an' the solitude an' the currents shiftin'. If all that's left to us is crabs an' whelks, I ent gooin' a do it. T'ent realistic n'more, MacLean.

MACLEAN (*quieter, even gentle, but no less intense*). I don't get it. Yoov a radar fer fish. What's 'appened t'yoo?

KEN. What's 'appened t'me? I'm scrap like my boot.

MACLEAN. You ent scrap.

KEN. Yeah.

*The two men are now very close to each other, talking with quiet intensity, excluding the women.*

MACLEAN (*with no conviction, only sadness*). If we can't find no fish, it's 'cause we ent lookin' in the right place.

KEN *shakes his head.*

. . . Yoo ent givin' in, boy, I won't 'ave it.

HILARY *sees the man from MAFF approaching from offstage.*

HILARY. Ah! 'Ere 'e is. At last!

SELIMA. Thank Christ.

*The rest of them look in the same direction, as the MAFF man comes closer.*

BILL *enters, in the uniform of a MAFF official: a cap, sturdy boots and a heavy winter coat. He carries a clipboard. He is now 66.*

BILL. Sorry to have kept you waiting. Bill Bretherton. Chief Inspector for MAFF. (*Checking the name of the boat against his notes.*) Now, this'll be 'The Mearston', yes?

*Lights out.*

## ACT THREE

### Scene One

*The year 1978 is projected onto the set.*

*A table that's been bleached by the sun dominates the action. On the table are a jug of wine, some satellite photos, a map, some folders and two briefcases.*

*The lighting suggests the scene is outdoors. The sun is beginning to set.*

*We are on a terrace on a farm, near the eastern shore of Sicily.*

*Occasionally, the sound of mechanical digging can be heard.*

*There are three men:* GAETANO *from Italy (late thirties),* JAN *from the Netherlands (mid-forties), and* BILL, *now fifty-two.*

*They have their jackets off and ties loosened, evoking the heat.* GAETANO *has a camera round his neck. They hold glasses of wine.*

GAETANO (*toasting*). Salute!

BILL. Salute!

JAN. Salute!

    *They all drink.*

    . . . Good trip?

GAETANO. Lucky. Few roadblocks. I avoided Palermo.

JAN. We only wait now for one more, the West German delegate.

BILL (*flicking through notes*). It's a pretty straightforward case.

JAN. We listen to what the farmer says and present our evidence. (*Pouring some more wine for* GAETANO *and himself.*) You have been on these delegations before?

GAETANO (*putting his briefcase on the table with the others*). No, actually, I was working with the Medicines Control Agency in Nancy. Fairly Dull. You've been working with CAP for a long time?

JAN. Me, yes. Our Head of Delegation is newer.

GAETANO. You don't look new.

BILL. Strangest middle-aged crisis of all time. I ran away to Europe to work on the Common Agricultural Policy!

GAETANO *laughs.*

. . . But I'm proud of what we do. Especially now with the Fraud Commission. I tell the team in Strasbourg: 'As the head of your delegation, I understand that our role is to create Europe.' The politicians pontificate, but we make it happen. On the ground. In the field. Getting our hands dirty.

JAN. That is the reason you give yourself to get up in the morning? To create Europe!

JAN *and* GAETANO *laugh.*

. . . Bill is our little Messiah. (*Teasing.*) Je bent onze kleine Messias! [You're our little Messiah!]

BILL. Hou op! [Shut up!]

JAN. A very lovely woman brought the wine. We'll ask her to show us around if she comes back.

GAETANO. Good.

BILL. It's a classic 'paper wheat' case, this. We've got the satellite photos here. Look.

GAETANO *looks over* BILL's *shoulder at the satellite photos.*

. . . We're here. You can see Messina. That's there. And that's the road. (*Pointing to areas on the photos.*) So all of that is lemon trees and all of that is olives. And that's peaches. You can tell by the colour and the pattern. Now, the subsidy claim form the farmer submitted to Brussels was for 2,500 hectares of durum wheat. Naturally, wheat gets the largest subsidy. Well, the entire farm's no more than 250 hectares, and there's not one sheaf of wheat growing anywhere, durum or otherwise. (*Indicating out-front.*) Orchards and olive groves as far as the eye can see.

MARCELLA, *the farmer's sister, enters. She's dressed fashionably, not for farming. She brings plates of food and more wine.*

MARCELLA (*to* GAETANO). Ma ché cazzo fai! Si tu ficchi pi cuomo posteggi si siguru cha cia li corna! [Fucking hell! If you fuck as badly as you park, it's not wonder you're a cuckold!]

GAETANO (*taken aback by this vulgarity*). Ma chi dici, signura? [Excuse me? What did you say?]

MARCELLA (*putting food in front of* JAN). Prego.

JAN (*inaccurately*). Gracias.

JAN *is physically attracted to* MARCELLA.

BILL. I feel almost guilty eating her food when we're going to close down her farm. What is this?

GAETANO. Sardine alla beccafico. Sardines a la fig-eaters, literally.

JAN (*mixing up his languages as ever*). Heerlijk! È delizione! [Gorgeous! It's delicious!]

GAETANO. See, the sardines are arranged to look like the little birds, the fig-eaters.

MARCELLA *stays, and* JAN *flirts with her through the following.*

. . . (*To* MARCELLA.) La vistu un beccafico? [Have you ever seen a figpecker?]

MARCELLA. Sì, navota nili mangiavamu, ma ora non ci ne chiù. [Yes, we used to eat them, but you don't see them any more.]

JAN. What is she saying?

GAETANO. She said you do not see them any more. Like many species, they have disappeared from Sicily. We used to eat them.

JAN. Maybe that is why they disappeared.

BILL. No, it's the effect of pesticides or a rise in monoculture more likely.

GAETANO. Really?

JAN. Don't show interest.

BILL. Yes. CAP only approves a very small selection of grain seeds. That rewards the most technologically advanced farmers. Improves the profit margin for the richer farmer. Messes things up ecologically.

JAN. I'm sorry, my colleague is boring. What I do not understand is why Bill works for the EEC. It makes him so unhappy! (*About* MARCELLA.) Look at this girl. God, zij is mooij! [God, she's beautiful!]

BILL. Behave yourself.

JAN. Plat flicker op, Bill. Je bent niet m'n vader! [Fuck off, Bill. You're not my father!]

GAETANO. Signura, puozzu taliari la masseria? [Would it be possible, Miss, to see over the farm?]

MARCELLA. Vua taliari ora? [You wanna see it now?]

GAETANO. Sì, grazi. [Yes, please.] She asks is this a good time to see the farm?

JAN. I think it would be very rude to disappoint her.

BILL. One of us better wait here for the German delegate.

GAETANO. Would you mind, Bill? I would love to cast my eye around. I think it was a mill in the past. The stream has diverted itself over there.

BILL. Oh yes.

GAETANO. I want to take some photographs of the place.

BILL. You go ahead.

JAN (*to* MARCELLA). Sì, Signora! Vamos!

MARCELLA (*allowing* JAN *to go ahead of her*). Prego.

JAN. Gracias.

MARCELLA (*laughing and following him off*). È spagnolo, imbecille. [That's Spanish, idiot!]

GAETANO *follows the others off, taking his camera with him, leaving* BILL *alone onstage.*

FRAU BETTENDORF *is heard arriving offstage.*

FRAU BETTENDORF (*offstage*). Guten Abend! Buona sera? Hello?!

BILL (*calling off*). Hello!

FRAU BETTENDORF *enters carrying bags. She is exhausted from travelling and preoccupied with her luggage, so she doesn't actually look at* BILL *for a while.*

FRAU BETTENDORF. You must be the UK man. I am so sorry to be so hopelessly late.

*Surprisingly, the German delegate speaks with a native upper-class English accent. After dealing with her bags, she retouches her make up and hair, or sorts through things in her bags, and looks at the view, still not bothering to clock* BILL.

. . . The Dutch and Italian delegates are here already, are they? I'm not normally late. But the whole journey's been ghastly. I've come from Frankfurt. Via London, to see relatives. And of course there was a baggage-handlers' strike, so I was sat like an idiot at Heathrow for years, and then it took the pilot three attempts at Punta Raisi to actually land on that damned strip of earth they call an airport.

BILL (*amazed, breathlessly*). Pippa?

FRAU BETTENDORF (*not hearing* BILL). Then the most chaotic train journey to Messina, which was madly packed and late and slow . . . And when I got there, the centre of town had been turned into an animal market. Impossible to find a taxi. It was like Noah's Ark. Turtles, puppies, goats, monkeys, you name it. God, this view's marvellous, isn't it? I love bougainvillea best of all, I think. (*Turning to* BILL.) I'm Frau Bettendorf. English, obviously. Married a German. Hello.

BILL. Pippa?

PIPPA (*properly looking at* BILL). My God! It can't be!

BILL. But . . . You've changed your name? (*Consulting the notes.*) We were expecting a Frau Bettendorf.

PIPPA. No, that's me!

BILL. I thought Axel's name was –

PIPPA. My God, yes! The last time I saw you I was about to marry Axel!

BILL. Didn't you?

PIPPA. No, I married Matthias.

BILL. And you were going to Heidelberg.

PIPPA. We live in Stuttgart! Hah! Eleven years. Two kids. Can you believe it?

BILL. Oh. (*Not meaning it.*) Great. Good.

PIPPA. Bill, how wonderful to see you!

PIPPA *instigates a hug.*

BILL (*tearfully*). You look exactly the same, Pippa.

PIPPA (*exploding with laughter*). Oh Bill! I look a hundred and five. What the hell are you doing here?

BILL. The same as you –

PIPPA. No! Don't tell me they're sending you off on these junkets now. When did you leave Number 10?

BILL. I applied to Brussels as soon as the ink on the Accession Treaty had dried.

PIPPA. Poor Bill. What did you do to deserve it?

BILL. I love it! I stayed in Downing Street for ages after you left. I was endlessly promoted and became more and more of a servant the higher I got.

PIPPA. God yes. I felt my life withering away in that awful gentleman's club.

BILL. How long have you been working for the Common Market?

PIPPA. Since I married. He's mostly in Strasbourg. We commute to Stuttgart for the weekends. I have some

languages. They get four for the price of one with me!
Unfortunately, not one of them is Italian!

BILL. Wouldn't do you any good here anyway. It's dialect. I
can't understand a word of it. The Italian delegate
thankfully does.

PIPPA *looks at* BILL, *shakes her head.*

PIPPA. I always asked after you to mutual friends. I assumed
you'd stay and work with your chum Teddy. He did well,
didn't he?

BILL *laughs ruefully.*

. . . But then, you know, time moves on; people stop
knowing people . . . How's the love life? I expect you've got
hundreds of girlfriends.

BILL. I'm fifty-two!

PIPPA. Well, is there someone special?

BILL. Oh yes.

PIPPA. Excellent! Who?

BILL (*unable to answer* PIPPA's *question*). Listen, have some
wine. Would you like some? You'll have to use my glass.

PIPPA. Sure.

BILL (*pouring wine*). I imagined what it would be like,
running into you again –

PIPPA. And here we are, in this beautiful place.

BILL (*pouring wine into one of the other glasses for himself*).
It was even better when the sun was still up.

PIPPA. Oh, it's glorious!

BILL. Salute!

PIPPA. Salute!

BILL (*avoiding* PIPPA's *eyes*). You should have a look at the
notes.

PIPPA (*moving to the table*). These they?

BILL. Yes.

PIPPA *looks at the notes, files and photos.* BILL *drinks wine and looks at the view, trying to pluck up the courage to declare his feelings.* BILL *will continue to drink steadily through the following.*

*As the sun has set, a fire that has been, almost imperceptibly, burning in the distance (out-front) has become more noticeable. It will grow in intensity towards the end of the scene, providing a strong light source.*

. . . (*Looking out-front at the view.*) This is where the Common Market was born, you know. Down there in Messina. Twenty odd years ago. The six Foreign Ministers started the process of transforming their 'Coal and Steel' union . . . Ironic, isn't it? They made it down there, and they're ripping it off up here.

PIPPA (*reading from the notes, and eating*). 2,500 hectares. It's audacious. Gosh, this fish is delicious.

BILL (*drinking*). You know what that fire is? Those farmers down there are burning peaches. Hundreds of thousands of beautiful peaches that no one wants. We subsidise farmers to grow them till they're perfectly ripe, then we subsidise them to destroy 'em.

PIPPA. What's the alternative? We dump the excess on the Third World and undercut the local farmer?

BILL. The alternative is we subsidise European farmers not to use all their land. But because we also subsidise the most technologically advanced, production actually goes up!

PIPPA. But the peasants here were starving at the end of the war. CAP has at least guaranteed them a reasonable wage. Damn, I've got sardines on these satellite photos.

BILL (*drinking*). The ones who run this farm are not what you'd call peasants.

PIPPA. You sound angry.

BILL. No, I'm . . . It really is marvellous to see you again, Pippa.

PIPPA. Don't drink any more, Bill. You'll go pop.

BILL. No, you're right. (*Drinks.*)

BILL *moves towards the table and* PIPPA.

. . . I hoped perhaps, moving to Europe, I'd find you again. And I have.

PIPPA (*moving away, taking a satellite photo with her, the better to see it in the setting sun*). The detail on these photos is amazing. (*Looks at* BILL.) I don't think I've ever before heard you criticise even one aspect of the Project.

BILL. It was easier to love from a distance.

PIPPA. Well, that's true of everything, isn't it?

BILL. Working inside it has been a real eye-opener. Even if Europe wasn't simply too diverse to regulate fairly, this is the most bizarre system. You know, we haven't actually been able to make one of these fraud cases stick. Paper olives in Thessaloniki. Barefaced bribes in Belgium. In Lincolnshire they worked out a rather tawdry little scheme to get paid twice for each cauliflower they grew. But in actually prosecuting these cases, we've been presented with one legal loophole after another. If I can't nail this one, Pippa . . .

PIPPA. It's only the Agriculture Policy. Don't take it personally.

BILL. I'm not saying I don't support the principle.

PIPPA. Can you hear what you sound like? Denis Healey! My God, you'll be telling me in a minute there's no way to reform it because of the French veto.

BILL. It's true!

PIPPA. But you're the most gung-ho federalist that ever existed. What happened?

BILL (*drinking*). It feels wonderful to tell the truth at last! I don't dare say this kind of thing in Strasbourg. It must be you! Your presence!

PIPPA. The wine more like.

BILL (*looks at his glass and shrugs*). You know, there was a report doing the rounds of the UK commission last month that said CAP costs more than it would cost to cover every square inch of Common Market land with top-quality carpet!

PIPPA. What a very English-sounding report.

BILL. It was Danish asherly . . . *actually*.

PIPPA. Oh, Bill, you've turned into a curmudgeonly middle-aged bureaucrat. Once you were flush with idealistic youth. The idea was perfect. Details were of no concern.

BILL. My God, you're right. Now all I see is details. Fiscal, mercantile, boring details. I bore myself with it.

PIPPA. Don't worry. It's a very English response to being in Europe. I've seen it again and again.

BILL. CAP made a kind of sense when the French could play the war victim, but to continue to justify it now, she's reduced to playing the role of spoiled child.

PIPPA. I'm ashamed of you.

BILL (*drinking*). Well, either *it* has to bend or *I* do. I've been about to snap, Pippa! Tell me about Matthias. Are you happy w–

PIPPA. Oh! You should come and visit us! It's fascinating there, Bill. You'd love it. Well, at least the Bill I used to know would. Before Britain joined the Common Market, Germany practically paid for CAP single-handedly, and they didn't complain. The thinking is completely different. The country itself has been a federation of states for more than a hundred years, so they're much more used to the give-and-take of federal politics. Westphalia doesn't insist on having its own currency; Bavaria doesn't want its own air force. They really can't understand why Britain drags its heels every time there's some initiative towards further integration.

BILL. Well, as long as the German economy continues to boom. What happens if you hit a recession?

PIPPA. As long as my adopted countrymen know that, per capita, the Dutch are paying more into the pot, everything'll be alright!

BILL (*drinking*). We're beginning to understand in England what the Welsh and the Scots have felt like for hundreds of years.

PIPPA. I'm not going to argue with you any more. We haven't seen each other for so long.

BILL. You're right. (*Summoning all his courage to broach the subject of his undimmed feelings.*) Pippa –

PIPPA. Listen. Bill . . . ? You don't think this could be a Mafia thing, do you?

BILL. Mafia?

PIPPA. It's large-scale stuff. Could it be?

BILL. The Mafia aren't interested in wheat, are they? Isn't it all cocaine and guns?

PIPPA. I hope so.

BILL. Strasbourg wouldn't have sent us to . . .

PIPPA. No, you're right.

BILL (*drinking*). They don't get involved with foreigners anyway. They just kill each other.

GAETANO *enters.*

GAETANO. It's fantastic. It is like a maze. Hello.

PIPPA. Pippa Bettendorf. West Germany.

GAETANO. Gaetano Tantillo. Italia. Piacere. [It's a pleasure.] It is an amazing structure. Odd alcoves, and rooms that suddenly end, or are cut into. Passages that lead nowhere. Landings halfway up a wall. The machinery for milling wheat is still there, underneath, but it is rusted. Totally useless.

BILL. Where's Jan? Is he coming?

GAETANO. I left him with that woman.

BILL (*drinking*). Well, that's the last we'll see of him tonight.

PIPPA (*eating again*). God, this is fabulous. Is this swordfish that's wrapped round the sardines? Bill, you'll have a terrific hangover if you carry on at that rate.

GAETANO. Ah! We are lucky. We do not have hangovers. Well, we do not have a word for it.

PIPPA. Listen – Gaetano, is it? – I was just asking Bill –

PIPPA *is interrupted by the entrance of* CICCIO
[*pronounced 'chee-cho'*]. *He is friendly and welcoming.*

CICCIO. Salutamu a tutti! [Good evening, everyone!]

GAETANO (*offering his hand to shake*). Buona sera, Signore.
Gaetano Tantillo.

PIPPA. Buona sera.

BILL (*focusing his thoughts again on the task ahead*). Buona
sera.

CICCIO (*shaking hands with* GAETANO). Benvenuti!
[Welcome!] Ciccio Cataldo. Prego accomodativi. [Please sit
down.]

GAETANO. Chisti sunnu personi della Communita Europea.
Chista è Pippa della Germania e Bill della Grande Bretagna.
[These are the EEC personnel. This is Pippa from Germany.
And this is Bill from England.] This is Ciccio, the farmer.

CICCIO. Mi fa piacere, chi vuliti sapiri?

GAETANO. He wants to know what we want to know.

BILL. Well, first of all we want to know does he receive our
guidelines and regulations?

GAETANO. Aviti ricevutu u documentu – l'istruzione della
Communita Europea?

BILL. We send them regularly –

CICCIO. Si, li ittau tutti.

GAETANO (*surprised*). He throws them all away.

*The delegates are startled.*

BILL. Why?

GAETANO. Pirchi?

CICCIO. Pirchi nun h'annu importanza.

GAETANO. Because they're irrelevant.

CICCIO*'s chumminess suddenly vanishes. He is stony hard;
his previous friendliness now seems to have been an act.*

CICCIO. Vinistivu cha pi dirimi chidru cha fare con la mia
masseria?

GAETANO. Have we come here to tell him how to run his farm?

PIPPA (*nervously*). No, not at all. We –

CICCIO. Io vi dicu chistu. (*Pointing.*) Dopo dru mare c'é il continente.

GAETANO. Listen. Anything beyond that sea there is the continent.

PIPPA. You know who he reminds me of, Bill?

CICCIO. Il continente è chidri chi viennu cha a dirimi chidru cha fare.

GAETANO. The continent is anything that comes onto the island that tells him what to do.

PIPPA. The English.

CICCIO. Non m'interessa si veni di Roma o Bruxelles.

GAETANO. He doesn't care whether that is from Rome or Brussels.

CICCIO. Si vinistivu cha pi essere li ma patruna, vuandri siti lu continente.

GAETANO. If we come here and want to be his boss, we are the continent.

BILL (*to* PIPPA). Yes! I see what you mean.

CICCIO *takes a revolver from his pocket and puts it on the table between him and the delegation, but closer to him and pointing at them.* PIPPA *emits a little scream. She and* GAETANO *are terrified.*

PIPPA. Let's get out of here.

GAETANO. Don't do anything quickly.

PIPPA. What about the Dutch delegate?

BILL (*drunk enough to be impractically indignant*). Now, wait a moment . . .

PIPPA. Be quiet, Bill.

CICCIO *lets the silence last. Then he becomes charming and expansive again.*

CICCIO. Dicimi pirchi u documentu é sbagliatu?

GAETANO. He asks what is wrong with his claim form?

BILL. He is claying for things . . . He is *claiming* for things he is not growing.

PIPPA (*to* BILL). Don't push it.

BILL. No! This won't do! (*To* GAETANO.) Tell him.

GAETANO. Tu riclami cosi cha non cresci. [You're claiming for things you're not growing.]

CICCIO. Non m'interessa un cazzu. (*Gestures with the back of his fingers flicked from throat to chin.*)

GAETANO. He doesn't give a fuck about that.

PIPPA. We should agree with whatever he says and get out of here.

GAETANO. I agree. We mustn't argue with him.

PIPPA. Tell him we'll reconsider our position and come back another time. Tell him we see his point, and if he'd be kind enough to –

GAETANO. Si, lu capiscinù – [Yes, they understand – ]

CICCIO (*interrupting aggressively*). Ascunta. Per mia chisti regole nun cuntanu.

GAETANO. He says he sees our rules as optional.

BILL (*recklessly, thinking that the argument is worth winning*). That is beside the point. This is the kind of reasoning that –

PIPPA. Bill! Enough! Stop. Don't provoke him, for God's sake.

BILL. Why the hell not? What have I got to lose?

PIPPA (*confused and frustrated*). You're being a fool. You always were a fool.

BILL. Well, then. (*Definitively.*) He can shoot me if he wants. I don't care any more.

PIPPA. At this moment I don't care if he shoots you either. But I care a whole lot about me.

BILL (*to* GAETANO). Tell him, it's not important what he thinks about the regulations –

PIPPA. You're the most naive person I've ever known.

BILL. But it's important he obeys them.

CICCIO. Chi dissi?

GAETANO. He's asking what Bill is saying.

BILL. Tell him.

GAETANO. Better not, I think.

PIPPA. Don't tell him!

BILL (*to* GAETANO). I order you, as head of delegation, to tell him what I said!

PIPPA. Oh, for God's sake!

GAETANO (*nervously*). Chidru chi vossia pensa, un ciavé importanza. [What you think is not important.]

CICCIO, *amazed that someone would be this impertinent, goes up to* BILL, *inspecting him closely, menacingly.*

CICCIO. Cuéstu maniaco del lavoro? Cuestu stacanovista.

GAETANO. He says who is this workaholic? This . . . 'Puritan', perhaps?

CICCIO. Oh come suffriti vuandri du Nord!

GAETANO. Oh, how you Northerners suffer!

CICCIO. Con i vostri forte apparenza e silenziose emozioni.

GAETANO. With your stoic nature and your silent emotions.

PIPPA (*finally getting it, to* BILL). Do you mean to tell me that all these years . . .

CICCIO *picks up the gun and aims it at the delegates.*

(*About the gun.*) . . . Oh my Christ!

GAETANO. Minghia! [Fuck me!]

CICCIO. Allura, non sappiti cu cu iucati?

GAETANO. Do you not realise what you are playing with?

CICCIO. Un sugniu sulu ia.

GAETANO. It is not just me.

CICCIO. Nun putiti changiare mai li cosi cha.

GAETANO. You will never change the way things are here.

CICCIO. Nuautri aviemu amici in tutti pusti.

GAETANO. We have friends everywhere. (*Understanding* CICCIO*'s implication, that they have stumbled into a Mafia situation.*) Oh my God.

PIPPA. Oh, no.

GAETANO. We have to be very, very careful.

CICCIO. Vini putiti iri, si mi diti cha viditi u frumientu crisci nella mia terra. Dumila cinqucientu ettere di frumientu.

GAETANO. He says we are free to leave if we agree that we see wheat growing on his farm. 2,500 hectares of wheat.

BILL. Now, wait a moment. This intimidation can't go unreported.

PIPPA. For Christ's sake, Bill, he's going to kill us.

BILL. If we just ignore this kind of threat, then the whole of CAP is undermined. Next thing, the entire European project –

GAETANO. This is something for the state. This is beyond our remit.

PIPPA. Yes, we can see wheat. For God's sake. Tell him.

GAETANO (*to* CICCIO). Sì sì, sicuramente. Nuaudri vidiemu u frumientu. [Yes, yes. Absolutely. We can see wheat.]

PIPPA. We can see wheat. Wheat as far as the eye can see.

GAETANO (*to* CICCIO). Frumientu, sì, frumientu. [Wheat, sure, wheat.]

*Aware that* BILL *is the troublemaker,* CICCIO *holds the gun to* BILL*'s head.*

CICCIO. É chidru? [And him?]

PIPPA. Just say it, Bill.

BILL. I want my objection registered.

PIPPA. It's registered! Now, for God's sake . . . You know as well as I do, the Fraud Commission's just public-relations pap. Tell him whatever he wants to hear.

BILL (*appalled*). Public-relations pap?

GAETANO. Listen to me very carefully, Bill. You cannot single-handedly –

BILL. Someone's got to stand up to them!

PIPPA. Is it worth more to you than your life?

BILL. At this moment I don't believe I have a life.

PIPPA. Absurd little man!

GAETANO. Bill. Please.

CICCIO *cocks the gun, still aiming it at* BILL'*s head.* PIPPA *screams.*

PIPPA. Just say it!

BILL (*breathing hard*). Only because you ask me to, Pippa. (*After a moment.*) OK. (*In agony.*) I see wheat. 2,500 hectares of wheat.

*Momentarily, the colour and noise of fire floods the stage.*

*With blackout comes the sound of the fire louder and louder.*

### Scene Two

TEDDY'*s Queen Anne home in the close of Salisbury Cathedral.*

*Projection: 1984.*

TEDDY *enters, bringing a guided tour of his property to an end. He is followed by* BILL.

TEDDY. That woman's a pest. Hasn't the faintest idea or understanding of the European vision. Rules and regulations; budgets, figures and sums. That's all she cares about. And what does she give us instead? War! Empty-headed nationalism. Reckless attempts to revive a dead dream.

BILL. But that was your idea, wasn't it? Reviving Britain's greatness.

TEDDY. In Europe, Bill! In Europe! Not charging about the South Atlantic in battleships, for God's sake. Makes my blood boil. Drink?

BILL. Lovely.

TEDDY. Whatever I say they rubbish. I've become the Trotsky of the Tory party. I'm an Unperson. It rather serves to make me think I must be right about everything. Ice?

BILL. Thanks.

*TEDDY finishes making the drinks. The nearby Cathedral bells chime the hour. TEDDY hands BILL his drink.*

. . . Thanks for agreeing to see me.

TEDDY. Just back for a break?

BILL. No, no, I'm back for good. Spent a decade filing reports for CAP only to have my findings buried.

*BILL knocks back his drink.*

. . . Teddy, the thing's impossible to enforce. It's anything but an even playing field. Sure, only relatively small percentages of the CAP budget go astray, but it represents billions in absolute terms.

TEDDY. Bad luck

BILL. Not done to criticise.

*The two men sit in silence for a moment, glowering at the carpet, contemplating their powerlessness.*

. . . I tried insisting that someone listen to my evidence and I was given three month's notice.

TEDDY. Really? They fired you? Too bad, old chap. Have another?

BILL. No, thanks, I'm . . . Didn't give the cause of Federation a good name at a tricky time. All the hatches are battened down tight, now Thatcher's attacking so strongly –

TEDDY. That bloody woman. She makes everything worse. You're better off out of it. She believes in Europe; at the same time she tries to kill the idea stone dead. When I think how hard I worked to get Pompidou on side . . . She has no rapport whatsoever with Mitterrand or Kohl. She's just rude to them. (*Getting himself another drink.*) There hasn't been a more significant time in Europe since the days of the Schuman Plan – Delors unveils the scheme to turn the Community into a Union, and all she can talk about is money. Bloody, bloody . . . shopkeeper's daughter.

BILL *gets up.*

. . . You know her tricks, Bill? She goes round specifically telling all the Ministries to enforce every European directive to the letter of the law with uncompromising rigidity, so that when she goes across to Europe for a summit, she can play up the fact that the British are the good boys of Europe, the least likely to defraud, the only ones to enforce legislation properly, while all the time she can say (*Doing an impersonation of Thatcher.*) 'No, no, no!' to everything new that comes up at the summit. She wants exemptions and derogations against everything, and now the bloody woman even wants a rebate against our contribution to the budget, as if greed itself were a policy –

BILL. I read you got *your* derogation.

TEDDY *finds himself looking at the back of* BILL, *who is looking out of the window. He doesn't know what* BILL *is talking about at first.*

. . . Staved off the Common Fisheries Policy.

TEDDY. Oh. Of course.

BILL. Temporarily. It would have expired a couple of years ago?

TEDDY. Yes, I suppose it would have done. Let me fix you another one of –

BILL. If you insist.

TEDDY *takes* BILL's *glass.*

. . . Though you pretended it was permanent.

TEDDY. What's that?

BILL. Your lie to Parliament. In the Commons.

TEDDY. Now listen here, old chap –

BILL. I followed events, Teddy –

TEDDY. That's a pretty serious charge, old boy. I have never lied to Parliament.

BILL. Not you, of course. *You* didn't lie. You got Geoff Rippon to lie for you. Before the Commons voted on whether to give you permission to take us in, back in '72, someone stood up and asked, 'Is the fishing derogation temporary?' Rippon replied for you and said it wasn't. He knew it was. You knew it was. But based on that lie, the Commons gave you your majority, and in we went. Do you honestly think they'd have gone for it if they'd known the truth?

TEDDY. What I've done is put us at the heart of Europe. Even if that bloody woman is trying to –

BILL. Europe? Whatever it is – a Community, a Union – it isn't Europe. It's a collection of a few Western –

TEDDY. The most powerful countries –

BILL. Sure, if you think Luxembourg's more powerful than . . . let's see . . . Poland or Turkey? It calls itself 'Europe'. Shamelessly arrogates the name. Defending the idea of a united Europe, I end up defending the Common Market! You criticise the thing, you're being anti-European. There's no room for an alternative vision –

TEDDY (*handing* BILL *a drink*). You're not saying that that's my fault too, are you?

BILL. Teddy, you didn't even give the people the choice. No referendum –

TEDDY. Referendum? That's not really the English way, is it.

BILL. Didn't it bother you? Doesn't it bother you? After all these years, there's still no grass-roots support for the thing! In this country, still no debate beyond the occasional invective that never rises above party-political squabbling. At least Wilson held the referendum you should have held. But if Delors succeeds in turning the thing into the European Union, will anyone explain to the people what that means? They voted to be in one thing in '75, and now they look around and find themselves in something completely different.

TEDDY. Whenever did your hero Monnet claim democratic accountability for the Project? 'The people need to be led,' he's always said. When real political integration's achieved, a constitution can be written, the people can be consulted and dutifully cast their 'Yes' votes.

BILL. Or 'No' votes.

TEDDY. Monnet still pulls the strings. I daresay that's what'll happen.

BILL. *You* should go and work there. You'd be much better at it than me.

BILL *knocks back his drink.*

TEDDY. Did you ask for this meeting so you could harangue me, Bill?

BILL. I've rather burned my boats, Teddy. Walking away from Whitehall and being given the push from Strasbourg. I can't afford to retire.

TEDDY *doesn't respond.*

. . . You could help me.

TEDDY. With what?

BILL *refuses to articulate further.*

. . . What sort of thing are you after?

BILL. I was thinking, with my experience in the field . . . You understand the sort of . . .

*Again* TEDDY *is silent.*

. . . It's a perfect view of the spire, isn't it?

*There is no answer from* TEDDY.

. . . Do you think you can?

*And again* TEDDY *leaves* BILL *hanging.*

. . . I'd be grateful.

*Lights out.*

## Scene Three

*We return to the beach in Suffolk. The boat is still moored on the shingle. The moon is up. The wind has not abated.*

*The action continues from a few moments after the last Aldston beach scene.*

*During this scene, BILL's accent very occasionally and very subtly shows signs of reverting to his native Suffolk. [Not specifically indicated in the script.]*

*BILL is a shadow of his previous enthusiastic self. He hides his disappointments behind bureaucratic efficiency.*

*He is handing some documentation to KEN.*

BILL. Fire's the usual method.

KEN (*amazed*). Fire?

BILL. Yes.

> MACLEAN, HILARY *and* KEN *are staggered.*

. . . Doesn't matter how you do it, as long as I'm satisfied that none of the constituent parts can be on sold.

KEN (*to* MACLEAN). We've protected 'er from all sorts, eh? I never thought t' see 'er burn while I were alive. (*To* BILL.) Yoo wouldn't know this. Fer 'undreds a years 'rown thee parts they'd burn a fish'man's boot on the beach if 'e died on land. Bury 'is body in the churchyard, and burn 'is boot on the beach.

> BILL *succeeds in remaining implacable.*

. . . Do you have paraffin?

BILL. I do. In the van. I'd have to charge you for it, though.

SELIMA. You enjoy your work, Mr Bretherton?

BILL. I have to tell you that in the eight years I've been at it, I've gained very little pleasure. Though I take some small consolation from the fact that I'm not long off retiring.

KEN. Let's jus' get this over. I got some paraffin in the shed up the beach. I'll get it.

KEN *exits.*

HILARY *turns on* BILL.

HILARY (*seething with fury*). What yoo gooin' a do? Build a marina 'ere for yachts, fill the town with bootiques an' arcades? Or maybe turn it into another artist's colony. Yeah, we need another one a them! Is that what the gov'ment wants?

BILL. The fish stocks are declining, Mrs Barry. We have to reduce fishing, cod especially.

HILARY. What yoo reckon these men're gooin' a do?

BILL. I'm afraid I don't know.

HILARY. Ent no other work for 'em 'rownd 'ere. Only area of the econ'my's expanding is bloody SEFRAS. Regulators and inspectors. Ministries and bureaucrats.

BILL. Now, let's not make this any more personal than –

HILARY. Shall I'll tell yoo somethin' else yoo don't know, yoo bastard. The cod goos to the bottom when it senses danger. It sees the bottom as protection, righ'?

BILL. I do know that, in fact.

HILARY (*exploding with pent-up rage*). Then what's the purpose o' destroyin' this boot? The factory ships ow' there 'ave rock 'oppers an' tickler chains, scopes and GPS. Them monsters know where the fish are to fifteen feet. The ocean floor they leave be'ind 'em is a desert.

MACLEAN. Tha's righ'.

HILARY. It's them 'oov made the cod commercially extinct. Them the EU licenses. Not these men in their two-man, forty-foot, wooden craft.

BILL. Our remit covers the domestic fleet. We're not in charge of the European Union's fishing policy.

HILARY. No, you jus' enforce it!

BILL. That's not –

HILARY. An' with a quota system that is so buggered . . .
Every quota system is, 'cause that ent the way fishin' works.

If yoo knew anythin' 'bowt fish'men yood know that quotas an' discards'll never work. A fish'man's brains ent built for thinkin' 'bowt how *little* 'e can catch.

BILL. It's the only means we have by which to control –

HILARY. An' 'oo comes up with the actual figures?

BILL. You'll have to take that up with the Ministry.

HILARY. The Minister ent returnin' my phone calls righ' now, sadly. But what good would it do me if 'e were? The decision were made in Brussels, weren't it? (*To* SELIMA.) Get this down. Everythin' might look the same in the papers an' on telly – there's still Ministers rushin' in an' out a revolvin' doors to very important meetin's and all that – but (*To* BILL.) these days your Ministry and all the others are no more than PR fronts to rubber-stamp what Brussels wants. The government don't work through primary legislation n'more. What we've got is government by regulation and decree. From Belgium.

BILL. I perceive your agenda.

HILARY. People don't realise 'ow undemocratic it is. It's a monster, created and run by some distant elite, and for 'em too.

BILL. The EU's a devilish monolith, populated by swarms of evil-doing Eurocrats trying to get one over on you.

MACLEAN. That's it!

BILL. I worked in Strasbourg for many years, Mrs Barry. I can tell you there are less bureaucrats working full time there and in Brussels combined than there are working for Nottingham City Council. I looked it up.

HILARY (*to* SELIMA). See? 'E's a mouthpiece for Europe.

BILL. I can assure you I'm not. You can say it's undemocratic, but hasn't it brought Spain and Portugal in from the undemocratic cold? Greece too. Rehabilitated them from military dictatorships to thriving liberal democracies without one shot being fired –

MACLEAN. What the 'ell 'as Greece and Portugal got to do with me?

HILARY (*to* BILL). Whatever yoo say, it's still some idiot in Belgium 'oo's decidin' all the quota figures for –

BILL. Now, listen, there's no need to make racist –

HILARY. I ent sayin' 'e's a *Belgian* idiot. I'm saying 'e's an *idiot*! Christ, 'e's got to be an idiot! He certainly don't know anythin' about fish! I've been to their office. I asked 'em. Not one on 'em 'ad ever been in a fishin' boat.

BILL. It's not a perfect system, but –

HILARY. An' they're deciding for every vessel in Europe. This month yoo can catch 'x' amount of 'a', as long as it's the right age an' the right length, but no 'b', 'c' or 'd'. How mad is that?! When yoo put yoor nets down – 'oo knows what's gonna come up?!

MACLEAN. Tha's righ'.

HILARY. Yoo tell a man 'e can catch a certain 'mount a fish, of a certain size, within a certain time – 'e ends up throwing more 'an 'alf his catch back overboard. It's too young. It's cod when it should be 'addock. 'E catches too much on what 'e's allowed. Back it goes. But once the fish is on the deck, it's dead.

MACLEAN. Tha's righ'.

HILARY. When you 'aul up a groundfish from fifty fathoms, the change in pressure bursts its swim bladder.

MACLEAN. 'E don't know nuthin'.

HILARY. Now yoov got millions a tons a perfectly good fish lying dead at the bottom a the ocean. Massive pollution on the seabed. They say it's six feet deep for miles an' miles in parts a the North Sea. It's a bigger ecological disaster than it was afore you started imposin' yoor flamin' quotas. They use quotas and discards the world over but only in the EU 'as it made things worse! 'Ow can tha' be possible?!

BILL. What? You want me to defend the CFP?

HILARY. It's yoor responsibility t'defend it if yoor destroyin' our lives with it.

BILL. Should have asked me twenty years ago.

HILARY. What the hell does that mean?

*She looks quizically at* BILL.

BILL. Oh, I can debate the hind legs off the EU and the CFP. Won't change anything here.

MACLEAN. Yoov got nuthin' to say about it?

BILL. Quite the contrary, if you insist.

HILARY. Yoo ent like the sort of MAFF people we usually deal with. Don't reckon none a them 'ave ever been outside Suffolk, let alone to Strasbourg. What were yoo doing owt there?

BILL. Working for CAP mostly.

HILARY. And?

BILL *doesn't respond.*

. . . I could've towd yoo it was a sham and saved yoo the trip.

BILL. I'm not here to take sides in an argument or defend CAP or the CFP.

HILARY. It was that bad, huh?

BILL. I understand your frustration. Believe me, I've heard it lots of times before. I found out in the field that the idea of Federal Europe appears a hell of a lot more attractive if you're living in the middle of it, not stuck out on an island on the edge. Like you are here. Do you think your husband's going to be much longer?

HILARY (*seeing there may be a chance of getting through to* BILL). Yoo understan' what we're tryin' a do here though, what we're tryin' a save. With the fish stocks the way they are, the future a the industry's gotta be wi' small boats like this one, not those fact'ry ships owt there.

BILL. But you'll never get the EU to go low-tech. It's whole purpose with fishing is to increase catch size and profitability, just like in agriculture. What? Do you imagine we should all go handlinin' again?

MACLEAN (*alert to the implications*). Yoo know 'bowt handlinin'?

HILARY. An' if we can't achieve that inside the EU, we should withdraw.

MACLEAN. Yeah! Britain ow' a Europe!

BILL. Don't give me that. It's a waste of energy arguing for withdrawal. It's not going to happen. Asking whether we'd be better off out of it takes attention away from the question you should be asking.

HILARY. Which is?

BILL. Well, for a start . . . If it's not fear of war any more, what drives the integration process these days? Where's the whole thing going? What's the point of it –?

HILARY. I'll tell yoo wha's the point on it. It's an end in itself. It's so the political elite can strut their stuff on a European stage, and then come 'ome and blame Europe when they have to force through decisions tha' ent popular. An' tha's why we should get owt on it.

BILL. I remember Ted Heath saying that he felt safe giving away our waters because fishermen weren't politically significant. He should have taken their wives into account.

SELIMA. Before I get permanent lockjaw and my hands fall off, I want to ask, can't we just pull out of the Fishing Policy if it's not working? I mean, stay in the EU, but –

HILARY. Bollocks. That ent 'ow it works.

SELIMA. Alright! Don't yell at me. I'm trying to –

HILARY. And I'm explainin'. Yoo never get anythin' back. Power only moves one way in Europe. From us to them. Oh yeah, the likes a John Redwood says, 'We'll go in and we'll jolly well tell them we're jolly well not having it!' I 'ave t' laugh. 'E's obviously never read the treaties the Union's founded on. None of it's renegotiable. The only thin' we can do if we want t' take anythin' back, or 'ang on to what we got, is t' withdraw completely. Iceland an' Norway are the only European countries with strategies tha' 'ave kept stocks 'ealthy and neither of them are in the EU.

BILL. How far did Mr Barry have to go for the paraffin?

HILARY. Don't yoo ignore me.

BILL. Alright! Iceland and Norway are special cases. They've got a lot of fish and relatively small populations.

HILARY. They're special cases 'cause they value their fisheries!

BILL. Look, you can't plan nationally when it comes to fish. Fish don't think about borders. We can't regulate them as if they do. And what's the alternative? You really think that Britain could possibly compete economically on its own – ?

HILARY. Don't yoo dare use the global economy argument. Look at Switzerland. It ent in any union an' its economy's growin' faster 'an France or Germany's.

MACLEAN. She's like a dog with a bone! Ent she grand?

BILL. No, it's too late to be having this conversation. Where the hell is Mr Barry? Too late and completely pointless –

HILARY. Yoo understan' thoo.

BILL. One perk of this job is that I don't have to have a conversation with you at all.

HILARY. Tell me yoo understan', you smug prick.

BILL (*swinging round on* HILARY). This isn't *my* fault! Of course! European mismanagement must be to blame for the decimation of all that cod! It couldn't possibly be because these fishermen here, and their fathers, and their fathers before them, have been overfishing these shores for centuries.

HILARY. I'm talkin' about *now*. We ent managin' the stocks in a sustainable way inside Europe *now*.

BILL (*his fury unabated*). And when they exhausted the fish round here, they plundered other countries. (*To* MACLEAN.) You're old enough to remember Iceland and the Cod Wars, I suppose . . .

MACLEAN. Remember? We was there! That's where Ken an' me met! Seventeen years owd, choppin' ice off our lines a foot thick, in a hundred-mile-an-'our gale. Fishin' and fendin' off the Icelandics twen'y hours a day. Not much yoo can tell me about them buggers –

BILL (*frustrated by* MACLEAN*'s verbosity*). Right! So what right have you to criticise other countries for having a share of our waters. (*To* HILARY, *about* MACLEAN.) They took their huge powerful steel boats and ran over the nets and lines of local fishermen –

MACLEAN (*about the Icelandic fishermen*). And then *they* got steel gun boots with underwater cutters to snip our warp. Rammed us with ruddy great ships reinforced for icebreakin'. My life! Bloody Icelandics; give us a right gooin' over.

BILL (*regretting that he let lose this torrent*). Yes –

MACLEAN. 'Ow much fish yoo reckon yoo could catch, playin' dodgem cars with icebreakers on the 'igh seas? –

BILL. Yes, but –

MACLEAN. Bloody terrible –

BILL. Yes, but the point is they had a right to defend their own territory!

HILARY. And we don't?!

BILL. I'm saying we've plundered enough. Maybe it's time to give something back.

MACLEAN. Why should we give anythin' back? Why shouldn't the *Spanish* give some'in? Get used to eatin' a different kinda fish for a start.

BILL. Why don't *we*? What's wrong with red fish, or pollock, or blue whiting? The Germans adapted to eating red fish easily enough when they left Icelandic waters.

MACLEAN. Why should we be like the Germans? Everyone 'ere loathes red fish.

BILL. I'm definitely not arguing with you if we're going to have to descend to the level of –

MACLEAN. And the Dutch'll eat anything! Get the bloody Spanish off our shores. Stop 'em takin' wha's ours!

BILL. Your problem's not the Spanish. They're newcomers in these waters.

MACLEAN. And they're makin' up for lost time fast! Spanish rogue pirates is what I see!

BILL. Their catch has been declining for years.

MACLEAN. They still 'ave the largest fleet.

HILARY. 'E's right. Three quarters the size on the rest a Europe's put together.

BILL. Maybe that's because they have the highest per capita fish consumption in Europe.

MACLEAN. *Of our fish!*

BILL. Well, where do you expect them to go for it? They have no good fishing grounds of their own.

MACLEAN. That's *my* problem? Yoo let Spanish ships invade the North Sea –

BILL. 'Let Spanish ships invade the North Sea!' It's the Armada all over again!

MACLEAN. Tha's righ'! It is!

BILL. You know, every time I start losing heart in the federal idea, I meet someone like you and my faith is restored. Every other country's on tight quotas just as much as you are: the Dutch, the –

HILARY. Every time there's quota cuts, we lose more 'an the Spanish. An' they're allotted a lot more top-end fish, like cod.

BILL. The Spanish aren't interested in your cod so much as your hake. But 'The Spanish are coming', so it's cod and chips and xenophobia. If we're going to have this argument get your facts right.

MACLEAN. I'll give you a fact. Thousands a years we've been fishin' cod from this coostline. Goo into the owdest church roun' 'ere, you'll see the shape of cod carved into pew ends. Not 'addock, nor anythin' else.

HILARY. Right. There's a peckin' order in fish. And cod is king. D'yoo 'ave any idea what it means to a fish'man when yoo tell 'im 'e can't fish cod. The damage yoor dooin'.

BILL. It's not me doing this.

MACLEAN. Well, who the bloody hell is?

BILL *is halted by this.*

BILL. If Mr Barry isn't back in a minute I'll be leaving. And you'll still owe the Ministry £147,000.

SELIMA (*packing up her bag*). I've got to go.

HILARY. No, stay till Ken gets back wi' the –

SELIMA *takes off the windcheater* KEN *lent her.*

SELIMA. I don't understand how it can take this long to get paraffin from his shed.

HILARY. I need yoor attention. I need yoo t' record this.

SELIMA *continues to take off the windcheater.*

. . . This deserves a witness, Selima.

SELIMA. If I miss the last bus I'm stranded.

SELIMA *holds out the windcheater, which* HILARY *refuses to take.*

HILARY. Put tha' back on. Yoor stayin'.

SELIMA. You can't order me about like that, Hilary.

HILARY. Get a taxi. Just stay!

SELIMA *drops the windcheater to the ground, starts to go and, glancing nervously at her watch, comes back.*

SELIMA. I'll tell you what I think. I love Europe. In fact, for my children's sake, I hope that one day Turkey will join, and –

HILARY. I ent anti-European!

SELIMA. What?!

HILARY. I'm just anti us being in it.

SELIMA. I know exactly what you people think of Europeans. Round here I hear it every day. They're untrustworthy, untroubled and too sophisticated for their own good. Well, that's *Western* Europeans. Eastern Europeans are just untrustworthy. At best. If you ask me, I'd rather have Europe any day than the States. All that awful sabre-rattling.

HILARY. That is such a lazy poin' a view. Dangerous too.

SELIMA. I'll tell you what's dangerous. (*Referring to* MACLEAN.) When he talks about losing his cultural identity –

MACLEAN. I never said nuthin' 'bowt my cultural –

SELIMA. All that business about red fish and Spanish boats. He's frightened because he thinks his identity is more important than anyone else's. I happen to disagree. I'll write up your story. I'll write exactly what I've seen. Goodnight.

HILARY. Yoo gotta get some shots a the burnin'!

SELIMA. I'll get something out of the library.

SELIMA *exits.*

HILARY. Stay!

SELIMA*'s gone.*

. . . Shit.

BILL. I've given Mr Barry more than enough time. You'll receive a letter from us outlining your options. I'm afraid neither of them is very appealing.

BILL *starts to leave.* MACLEAN *gets in the way.*

MACLEAN (*to* BILL). Yoor from round 'ere, ent yer?

*This is a question* BILL *has been dreading.*

BILL. I am. (*Starts to leave again.*)

HILARY. Wha'?

MACLEAN (*standing in* BILL*'s path*). 'Eard it in yoor voice.

BILL. Did you?

MACLEAN. Where'bouts?

BILL. I was born here, in Aldston in fact. Maitland Road.

MACLEAN. Yoo related t' Tom Bretherton?

BILL. He's my brother.

MACLEAN. 'E worked for Harrison's?

BILL. In the accounts department. And before that for Vincent's as a deckie.

MACLEAN. Yeah, I know 'im. Retired now. He paid our wages when we was on the trawlers.

BILL. That would make sense.

MACLEAN (*light dawning*). Yeah, you was the Bretherton that wen' away. (*Thinking this is the breakthrough they've been looking for.*) Well, fer God's sake, boy, let's forget this stoopidity and go to the pub an' talk like 'ooman beings to each other over a pint.

HILARY. Ent no purpose, MacLean. 'E's 'ere t' destroy us. (*To* BILL.) 'Ow many?

BILL. What?

HILARY. Boots yoo destroyed?

BILL. A fair few.

MACLEAN. But yoor one o' us.

BILL. I'm sorry.

MACLEAN (*appalled*). One Suffolk man t' another. Is there n'more in yoo 'an tha'?

BILL *doesn't respond.*

. . . You're a traitor, Bill Bretherton.

BILL. I have tried.

HILARY. What 'ave you ever done for this place but 'elp destroy it?

BILL *remains silent.*

MACLEAN (*incensed*). She asked yoo a question!

BILL (*to* MACLEAN). Take it easy.

MACLEAN. Wha' 'ave yoo ever done?

BILL. I don't have to answer your –

MACLEAN (*physically grabbing* BILL). Listen, yoo rotten twot! She asked you –

BILL (*to* HILARY, *intimidated*). Calm your bullyboy down.

MACLEAN. No! I wanna know!

BILL (*shouting back at* MACLEAN). I'm not a fisherman like you. I left here because there was nothing for me. But it doesn't mean I don't love this place like you do. Doesn't mean that I don't feel the same as you about what's happening.

HILARY. Yoov got a blinkin' clipboard and a safe little job. Don't yoo try an' make me feel sorry for yoo.

BILL. I'm not holding myself up as a hero.

HILARY. Good, 'cause you ent one.

MACLEAN *lets* BILL *go*.

BILL. I admit what I did wasn't enough. How could it be? I'm just a civil servant!

HILARY. I've collected scores a cases, jus' from rownd here, where lives are ruined and businesses destroyed by regoolators an' civil servants. Don't think yoor doin' yoorself noo favours by hidin' behind 'just a civil servant'.

BILL. What the hell do you want from me?

BILL *realises that he won't convince them.*

. . . Listen. What's given away is gone. We have to accept it.

HILARY. I do not 'ave to accept it.

BILL *moves towards the boat and leans on it. He is exhausted.*

KEN *reappears. He is standing motionless upstage with a large can of paraffin in each hand. If anything, he's even steelier now, more impenetrable. The others register his presence.*

KEN (*with focused ferocity to* BILL). Get yoor fucking hand off my boot.

BILL. Now, come on, let's keep this reasonable, Mr Barry.

*Nevertheless,* BILL *moves away from the boat. He galvanises what strength he has left.*

. . . If you're ready to proceed, I need you to sign one last piece of paper.

*Consciously controlling his breath,* KEN *puts down the paraffin cans, and walks over to where* BILL *holds out the clipboard and a pen.*

KEN *signs, gives* BILL *back the pen.*

KEN. Yoov regoolated us ow' of existence.

BILL (*who's had enough of the blame*). Welcome to the real world, Mr Barry; Forms and figures, compromises and responsibilities.

KEN. I 'ave tried to make it work. I 'ave dealt with yoor forms. The consequence on failing is too big. This is me life we're talkin' 'bout.

MACLEAN (*to* BILL). I hate yoo, yoo scum. (*To* KEN.) 'E's Tom Bretherton's brother. 'E's a traitor to 'is own people.

KEN *looks at* BILL.

BILL. I didn't intend this. This is the opposite of what I intended.

MACLEAN. Then don't do it!

BILL. You won't believe me probably, but I've sacrificed a lot, and compromised a friendship that was very important to me.

HILARY. Anyone notice?

BILL. I can't fight this system! I am not big enough!

KEN (*quietly, but directly at* BILL). Pathetic.

BILL *feels the force of this attack because he knows there is truth in it.*

. . . Let's 'ave done with talkin'. Yoo got a job to do, jobsworth. Watchin' me burn my boot. (*To* MACLEAN.) You gonna help me with this paraffin or what?

MACLEAN. No. An' I ent watchin' yoo do it neither. I'm gooin' a do some fishin'. I don't reckon anyone's gooin' a stop me.

KEN *starts to move round the boat, splashing paraffin against it as he goes.*

BILL. Mr Barry.

KEN *stops, but holds the paraffin can ready to continue.*

. . . This is absurd.

KEN (*to* BILL). I don't blame yoo.

HILARY. Yoo should.

KEN. We're all the same. Just dooin' our jobs.

KEN *comes right up to* BILL *and speaks slowly and firmly into his face. It's half an exoneration, and half an accusation of impotence.*

. . . It's nothin' to do with yoo.

BILL *registers the accusation rather than the exoneration.*

KEN *returns to splashing paraffin on the boat, till he's out of sight.*

HILARY (*to* BILL). That's it?! That's all there is?

KEN *comes back into view and climbs the ladder onto the prow. Once on the prow, he continues to splash paraffin around, and disappears out of sight again.*

MACLEAN *has picked up a fishing line and basic gear.*

MACLEAN. It's a full moon tonigh'. Great for fishin'. (*Slinging his arm round* BILL's *shoulder in a mock-pally/aggressive way.*) Yoo know why?

BILL (*his mind on himself*). Err . . . no.

MACLEAN. Front side on the moon yoo get small males. On the full moon the catch switches over an' the females completely lose their 'eads. They're larger than the males too, feedin' and carryin' on without carin' 'bout the consequences.

MACLEAN *exits, along the beach.*

HILARY *has become concerned because* KEN *hasn't reappeared on the prow.*

HILARY (*calling off*). Ken?

BILL (*to* HILARY). What is it? What's wrong?

KEN *reappears on the prow, and, in one movement, lifts the ladder up off the ground, hauling it on-board.*

HILARY. What yoo doin'?

KEN *towers over the others on the beach. He has the can of paraffin in one hand and an old rag in the other. He is staring down at them, grim-faced. He pours paraffin over the boat, on which he's standing.*

BILL. Better put the ladder back, and get down now, Mr Barry.

HILARY (*horrified*). Ken?

KEN *pours more paraffin.*

. . . Ken, come down. Please. Fer God's sake. We'll sort it out. (*With rising hysteria.*) Wait, Ken. Wait. I don't understan', love. Why?!

BILL. Please, Mr Barry.

KEN *drops the can, now empty, onto the deck of the boat, and takes a lighter out of his pocket.*

HILARY. We'll work i' ow'; we'll fin' a way. Other people 'ave. We can.

KEN. Yoo deal with yoor other people. Yoo run aroun' savin' ev'ryone and ev'rythin'.

HILARY. But it's all about yoo. Yoor me husband. There wouldn't be a campaign without yoo.

KEN *doesn't reply.*

. . . Just come down, Ken.

KEN. I ent strong enough. I got to be yoor 'usband, who brings 'ome the catch, or I can't be nothin' at all.

KEN *lights the rag and holds it over the paraffin-soaked deck on which he stands. It burns.*

HILARY. No!

KEN *drops the flaming rag onto the deck. Fire leaps up.*

*Blackout.*

*We hear an enormous explosion rippling into life.*

## Scene Four

*A projection tells us it is 2006.*

BILL *is now eighty years old. With him is a Catholic* PRIEST. *They are on the beach in Aldston. The beach is the same as before except without* KEN *and* MACLEAN'*s boat, or any evidence of fishing.*

*It's a bright, warm summer's day. The sound of a distant arcade and noisy children can just be made out.*

BILL. He wasn't your normal politician.

PRIEST. How so?

BILL. Had a really odd diet.

PRIEST. What do you know about that?

BILL. Only ate eggs and lettuce. Nothing else. Not much more comes to mind, I'm afraid.

PRIEST. Unfortunately there are very few people who are still with us who knew him at all, so –

BILL. He prayed a hell of a lot.

PRIEST. Right! Those campaigning for his canonisation maintain that he was a visionary statesman precisely because he was a Christian; that he used his faith as the engine for political action. The German Chancellor Adenauer referred to him as a priest in a suit.

BILL. And he's going to be called 'Blessed'? Give me a break. Blessed Robert, the French Foreign Minister? Hang on. If he's going to be a saint, doesn't he need to have performed miracles?

PRIEST. Well now, there's a separate panel of five medical experts who examine claims of miraculous cures.

BILL. And? Don't tell me people are saying he's –

PRIEST. There is, as yet, no record of his actual intercession in the lives of –

BILL. You don't say.

PRIEST. In fact, His Holiness is exploring ways in which the miracle clause might be circumnavigated.

BILL. What?!

PRIEST. Or would you perhaps acknowledge that the reunification of Europe after the war was itself miraculous?

BILL. But you're not suggesting Schuman was responsible for that, are you?

PRIEST (*missing the point*). Well, Rome is exploring the possibility of creating *three* new saints. Alcide de Gasperi, who was Prime Minister of Italy at the time, and Konrad Adenauer of Germany. Along with Robert Schuman from France.

BILL. Nice and fair. One of each. Who are they going to have from England? Ted Heath?

PRIEST. No, I don't, er, believe, in fact, that the United Kingdom –

BILL. Of course not!

PRIEST. You seem upset by this, Mr Bretherton. Perhaps –

BILL (*pointing*). You see that?

PRIEST. What?

BILL. Language School. Used to be Harrison's. Made ice, repaired boats in the back. All my nephews worked for Harrison's. Now it sells hats.

PRIEST. And some quite charming watercolours I noticed as we –

BILL. What of?

PRIEST. Boats mostly.

BILL (*opening his arms wide to take in the whole beach*). Do you see any boats?

PRIEST. Well, no, actually –

BILL. If what Schuman did, or in fact didn't do, is miraculous, then why is this place dead?

PRIEST. Perhaps we can return to the main point. In terms of finding a way around the miracle clause, His Holinesses sees a great opportunity in the recent French and Dutch votes against the Constitution.

BILL. What? What's the connection?

PRIEST. Austria's keen to begin the redrafting process –

BILL. The Constitution?

PRIEST. Yes.

BILL. Of course, when it comes to referenda, the EU has never been one for taking no for an answer –

PRIEST. And His Holiness is keen for the redrafted Constitution to set out clearly the Christian origins of the European Project –

BILL. I don't get it. What the hell's the Constitution got to do with Pope Benedict?

PRIEST. His Holiness understands that de Gasperi, Adenauer and Schuman constructed the foundation of the European Community on the rock of the Christian Church.

BILL. I don't believe that's true.

PRIEST. Schuman himself believed passionately that the Union of States is a design not only of human beings but of God. The flag – twelve stars – a Christian symbol representing the Virgin Mary's halo –

BILL. No. There were twelve stars because there were twelve member states at the time.

PRIEST. The European Commission has stated that twelve is taken from the number of the apostles and the sons of Jacob.

BILL. No more than it was taken from the number of months in the year or signs in the zodiac. Now negotiations have begun for Turkish accession, you can't have the EU pretending it's a Christian club –

PRIEST. Yes, Turkey makes it imperative we move fast. If the Vatican can ensure that any new Constitution directly credits the Christian faith as its inspiration and foundation, then His Holiness could find it relatively easy to overlook his concern about the need for actual miracles –

BILL. What?! The Pope's gonna trade? If the Constitution
defines itself as a Christian –

PRIEST. – pays due homage to the historical facts of its
Christian beginnings –

BILL. – then the Pope'll drop the miracle clause and canonise
the buggers?!

PRIEST. Europe is a relatively recent term, let's not forget.
Christendom was its original name.

BILL. Up till the Age of *Enlightenment*, yes. So, as soon as
there's a chance for Turkey, you lot move into action. What
won't you do to make sure we remain a frightened little
*cordon sanitaire* against Islam? Small and smug and rich
and frightened.

*BILL walks away, in disgust. A final thought. He turns back
to the PRIEST.*

. . . All of it's irrelevant anyway.

PRIEST. What is?

BILL. You've got the wrong man. Tell your Pope to do his
history homework. If he's going to canonise anyone, he
should canonise Monnet.

PRIEST. Monnet? Who's Monnet?

BILL. He wrote the plan. He created the Common Market. He
was the force behind the creation of the EU. Not Schuman.
Back-room boy. Like me. No one remembers him. Not even
a road or a building named after him in Strasbourg or
Brussels. But he was there every step of the way. Don't
suppose the Pope'll be much interested in him though.
Wasn't much of a Catholic.

*The PRIEST is baffled.*

. . . Now, where did we leave the car?

*BILL wanders off miserably, leaving the PRIEST behind.*

*Lights out.*

*The End.*

# AFTERWORD

## Afterword

There were several reasons and sources of inspiration for writing *The Schuman Plan*.

One theme emerged out of my lifelong love of Europe and things European. This started at an early age with music. I couldn't understand why my fellow countrymen didn't appreciate European popular music, indeed why 'Euro-pop' is a term of abuse. After all, it was all I wanted to listen to. Over ten years ago I wrote a play called *EuroVision*, which celebrated that.

Meanwhile, as a freelance director I found myself living for long periods of time on the continent. Sweden, for example, was where I happened to get regular work in the '90s. I also lived in Amsterdam for eighteen months, and Rome for a year. I thought of myself as a European – as much from love and respect for the continent's priorities and style as it was taking a stand against British jingoism and parochialism, which have always repelled me.

I'm sure I'm not saying anything controversial when I say that, broadly speaking, I find my fellow Brits xenophobic, condescending and/or frustratingly indifferent when it comes to Europe, though they like the continent for holidays. Whereas I learned, for example, what Europe Day was and what it means, here in England Europe Day continues to be regarded as a joke, if it's acknowledged at all. (By the way, it celebrates the anniversary of Robert Schuman's broadcast on French radio when he unveiled the Schuman Plan to the French.)

So when I came to write a new play in 2004 I decided to find a way to explore and dramatise Britain's anti-European feelings. I wanted to get to grips with both the ultra-nationalist United Kingdom Independence Party's brazen xenophobia and also the political establishment's brand of aloof prevarication and half-hearted engagement.

I had a grand conception of a piece that could draw a map of Europe through various snapshots of particular, widely-scattered places over the last eighty years or so. As I started the research, though, I realised I was creating a play that would run about eleven hours. So I refined my structure down to something more manageable, deciding to tell a story 'only' about Western Europe over the last fifty years. (An Eastern European story is the next thing I'm writing.)

I had long wanted to tell the tale of the life of a civil servant, so it seemed like the perfect opportunity to have one as my protagonist. This was partly I suppose because my father was a civil servant all his working life. I wanted to explore the effective limitations of a man's public power, when that man is intelligent, idealistic and hard-working. Through using a visionary, though lowly placed government employee, I intended to dramatise how a man might deal with being a small cog in a big machine.

On 1st May 2004, as I was starting work on the play in earnest, ten new countries acceded to the EU, including eight ex-Soviet states. On that day, the cruel and unnatural division between East and Western Europe that had been upheld for nearly sixty years effectively ended. It was, it is hoped, the real end of the Second World War. At night, fireworks punctured the dark European sky. From one end of the continent to the other, there were street parties, spontaneous or highly regimented. Traffic was brought to a standstill. Speeches were made by anyone who could get their hands on a microphone. It was a cause of mass celebration and saturation television coverage. Tens of thousands packed the main squares of the accession states' capital cities: Warsaw, Tallinn, Riga, Budapest, Prague, Vilnius, Nicosia, Ljubljana, etc. And in the old West too, the epochal significance of this reunification was marked with frenzied partying into the small hours: Paris, Madrid, Copenhagen, Dublin, Stockholm, Lisbon, Rome, Helsinki, Amsterdam, Berlin. At home in London, on that Mayday evening in 2004, I turned on the television. I flicked though all the stations and found nothing. Nothing at all. And as midnight chimed and the fireworks exploded all over continental Europe, BBC1 was showing a re-run of an old Jim Davidson gig.

I feel anger and shame about this country's relationship with its neighbours. And the Jim Davidson show confirmed my feelings that there might be a need for a play of this sort, at least to balance things out a bit. Anyway, I needed to write one, to get a few issues off my chest! There aren't many plays about Europe. Davids Greig and Edgar have embraced it. Tom Stoppard's new play, *Rock 'n' Roll*, takes on the subject. But what I wanted to do was explore specifically Britain's attitude to the rest of the continent. I am not aware that this has ever been explicitly tackled in dramatic form.

As I researched more, I found a wealth of startling material, enough to keep me busy writing plays about various aspects of Europe for the rest of my life, if that's what I wanted to do. I was confronted with the fact that Britain has a rich history of standing apart from the continent, using it and abandoning it when it stops being useful. Attlee, Wilson, Thatcher and Blair have merely been rehearsing old scripts. I understood that Blair, arguing for intergovernmentalism over federalism, directly links himself with Attlee fifty years earlier, but I was unaware that one could draw a straight line back from Blair to mediaeval England over 700 years ago, in this country's relationship with the continental Hanseatic League. I did not know, when I started work on the play, that a United Europe is not a twentieth-century invention, *pace* Napoleon, Attila the Hun, etc.

While researching the fishing industry, I read, in Mark Kurlansky's book *Cod* (Vintage, 1999) that, many hundreds of years ago, the Hanseatic League proposed something very similar to the Common Market and the EU. It had started in Lübeck, Germany, apparently, to protect the interests of the merchant classes in northern German towns and to regulate and control trade. The League achieved this by managing the mouths of the rivers that ran north from Central Europe. This highly successful so-called 'fellowship' spread fast and included London by the end of the thirteenth century. A century later there were chapters as far afield as Iceland, Latvia, the Ukraine, and Venice. It was, Kurlansky reports, universally popular. It stood up against the abuses of kings, stopped piracy, dredged channels and built lighthouses. In England, Hanseatic League members were called 'Easterlings'. From which, allegedly, the word 'sterling' comes, meaning 'of assured value'. But the League started abusing its powers. It became ruthless in defending its trade monopolies. It became so unpopular that mobs rose up in England and hunted down Hanseatics, killing anyone who couldn't say 'bread and cheese' with an English accent.

As I write this, we are living through the dying days of Britain's presidency of the EU. Blair has just completed a deal with the other twenty-four member countries, which finalises the budget for the next few years. No doubt Britain and other member states have a lot to complain about in terms of EU abuses of power, unfairness in how the budget is financed and the many idiocies of the Common Agricultural Policy, but it was amazing to see Blair and his negotiating team retreading the familiar ground of wanting Europe to develop in Britain's own image (with the expansion of markets in the east, limited social provision, etc.) and refusing to pay for it. (It was also frustrating to hear Jack Straw allowing himself to be ruder about his negotiating partners than he surely would be about colleagues in any other international forum, when he publicly referred to the difficulties of achieving agreement between all the members states as being 'like herding cats'.)

Like Thatcher before him, Blair sometimes pulls off the visionary speak of Europe. In the EU Parliament last month he said to a group of UKIP MEPs sitting behind Union flags, 'You sit with our country's flag. You do not represent our country's interests. This is the year 2005, not 1945. We are not fighting each other any more. (*Pointing to other MEPs.*) They are our colleagues and partners; and our future lies in Europe.' This, bar the years, could be Ted Heath. It could not, however, be Clement Attlee. So maybe things have moved on a bit.

Thirty years ago, Britain found itself in the same spot that Turkey's in now. Once again France was the chief enemy to a new accession state. Chirac's (and Merkel's) accusations against Turkish entry had their equivalent in de Gaulle calling a halt to Britain's ambition. He had the nerve to point out our European ambivalence, and vetoed Britain's membership of what was then the Common Market. Twice. He saw that Britain wanted 'in' in order to control, not to contribute. He identified the UK's not entirely honourable motives: wanting to get the best of both worlds – a special relationship with the USA *and* the trade advantages Europe has to offer – without exclusively committing to either. His judgement that Britain was 'not European enough' echoed Jean Monnet's prognosis of fifteen years earlier.

In fact, de Gaulle was amazed that Britain had twice gone so far down the application path, thus necessitating, after years of intricate manoeuvres and back-room deals, his last-minute veto. (Some people see a kind of echo of this brinkmanship and bluff-calling in Blair and Chirac's diplomatic manoeuvrings over the referenda on the EU Constitution.)

Many asked why, knowing Britain's predilections, de Gaulle hadn't stopped the whole process earlier on. A very French story went around at the time about de Gaulle being like the suitor who insisted he must see the girl naked before he would agree to marry her. Then finally, when she stood stripped before him, he objected to the shape of her nose. De Gaulle only had to use his veto because Britain had come so close to success. He had no idea we'd be prepared to strip so far!

Of course, Britain's not the only country in which domestic nationalism has put the brakes on the European federal process. Since the 'No' votes in France and the Netherlands last summer, it has been much easier for EU statesmen to openly express Euro-sceptic views. Austria's quite shameless in this regard, especially in its anti-Turkish position. And as far as Britain is concerned, having, over the years, ditched our popular culture in favour of an American imitation, I suppose some would argue that it's only natural we don't want to hand over our political and financial autonomy to Europe as well. (It surely isn't a coincidence that while we've lost all of our folklore tradition and any sort of healthy nationalism of the kind so apparent in many other European countries, Britain is the most sceptical member of the Union, primarily keen to allow EU membership to ex-Soviet European states in order to impede federation, and have more like-minded countries on-side.)

The more I researched, the more intrigued I became by the 'anti' argument. And I came to realise, just as the character of Bill does in the play, that perhaps my slavish adherence to the European party line was as blinkered as many of my countrymen's blind suspicions about anything that comes from beyond the English Channel.

The undemocratic nature of the Union's decision-making processes, its unaccountability (demonstrated, for example, by its high-handed take on referenda results in Denmark and Ireland), the adoption of the trappings and emblems of state (the flag, the anthem), its arrogation of the word Europe (when until recently it was nothing of the sort), made me start asking lots of questions.

And in asking those questions I was forced to ask questions about what the purpose of the EU is now. What had been a European Coal and Steel Community has become (via the Common Market, the EEC, and the EC) the EU: something other than what we were offered. I discovered that today its *raison d'être* revolves around its application of 'Soft Power'. This refers to the EU's ability, through the promise of greater prosperity to its new and prospective members, to play alchemist and change dictatorships to democracies without a shot being fired (cf. the US approach: 'Hard Power'). It was achieved with Greece, Spain and Portugal. It's being achieved with Turkey, the Ukraine, the Baltic and much of the Balkans, etc. In this way, so called 'special relationships' with countries currently on the fringe of the fringe of the EU may very well be doing more to help bring Middle Eastern governments into the Liberal Democratic fold. More than invasion, bombs and torture, anyway.

However, partly because I didn't want to write a play that would be out of date before opening night, I decided to write from a historical perspective. So today's rationale for the EU is not really part of *The Schuman Plan*. I am more concerned with its rationale fifty years ago. And through, for example, describing Britain while she was in the same position Turkey now finds herself in (i.e. an applicant country), I hope to throw some light on the present complexities of the European processes. Similarly, a long-term view of the Common Agricultural and Fisheries Policies can perhaps give a better perspective on things, as a new generation of politicians gets to grips with these aspects of life in Europe, and serve as a reminder of how long we've been engaged in the struggle, and how little the dynamics of it have changed.

*Tim Luscombe, January 2006*